Ms. Warner

A Treasury of
Presidential Quotations

WILLIAM J. FEDERER

Library of Congress Catalog Card Number 96-96840
ISBN 0-9653557-0-5

It would be peculiarly improper to omit, in this first official act, my fervent supplications to that Almighty Being who rules over the universe.

Thursday, April 30, 1789, First Inaugural Address.[1]

1st
President of the
United States
(1789-1797)

George
Washington
(1732-1799)

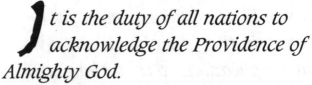

It is the duty of all nations to acknowledge the Providence of Almighty God.

Saturday, October 3, 1789, in a Proclamation of a National Day of Thanksgiving.[2]

I, George Washington, President of the United States, do recommend…a day of public thanksgiving and prayer, and on that day to meet together and render sincere and hearty thanks to the Great Ruler of Nations.

Thursday, January 1, 1795, in a Proclamation of a National Day of Public Thanksgiving and Prayer.[3]

1st
President of the
United States
(1789-1797)

George
Washington
(1732-1799)

5

George
Washington
(1732-1799)

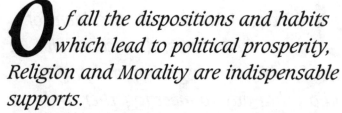 *f all the dispositions and habits which lead to political prosperity, Religion and Morality are indispensable supports.*

Monday, September 19, 1796, in his Farewell Address.[4]

***M**ay that Being who is supreme over all, the Patron of Order, the Fountain of Justice, and the Protector in all ages of the world of virtuous liberty, continue His blessings upon this Nation.*

Saturday, March 4, 1797, in his Inaugural Address.[5]

2nd
President of the
United States
(1797-1801)

John
Adams
(1735-1826)

Beseeching Him at the same time, of His infinite grace, through the Redeemer of the World, freely to remit all our offenses, and to incline us by His Holy Spirit to that sincere repentance.
Friday, March 23, 1798, in a Proclamation of a National Day of Humiliation, Fasting, and Prayer.[6]

That they call to mind our numerous offenses against the Most High God, confess them before Him with the sincerest penitence, implore His pardoning mercy, through the Great Mediator and Redeemer.

Wednesday, March 6, 1799, in a Proclamation of a National a Day of Humiliation, Fasting, and Prayer.[7]

2nd
President of the
United States
(1797-1801)

John
Adams
(1735-1826)

I t would be unbecoming the representatives of this Nation to assemble for the first time in this solemn temple without looking up to the Supreme Ruler of the Universe and imploring His blessing.

Saturday, November 22, 1800, in his Fourth Annual Address to Congress, which began the first session of Congress in the new Capitol of Washington, District of Columbia.[8]

Acknowledging and adoring an overruling Providence, which by all Its dispensations proves that It delights in the happiness of man here and his greater happiness hereafter.

Wednesday, March 4, 1801, in his First Inaugural Address.[9]

3rd
President of the
United States
(1801-1809)

Thomas
Jefferson
(1743-1826)

hilst we devoutly return our thanks to the beneficent Being who has been pleased to breathe into them the spirit of consolation and forgiveness, we are bound with peculiar gratitude to be thankful to Him that our own peace has been preserved.

Tuesday, December 8, 1801, in his First Annual Message to Congress.[10]

When we assemble together, fellow-citizens, to consider the state of our beloved country, our just attentions are first drawn to those pleasing circumstances which mark the goodness of that Being from whose favor they flow and the large measure of thankfulness we owe for His bounty.

Wednesday, December 15, 1802, in his Second Annual Message to Congress.[11]

3rd
President of the
United States
(1801-1809)

Thomas
Jefferson
(1743-1826)

3rd
President of the
United States
(1801-1809)

Thomas
Jefferson
(1743-1826)

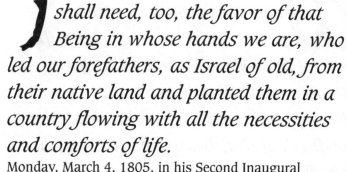

I shall need, too, the favor of that Being in whose hands we are, who led our forefathers, as Israel of old, from their native land and planted them in a country flowing with all the necessities and comforts of life.

Monday, March 4, 1805, in his Second Inaugural Address.[12]

14

*I*n these my confidence will under every difficulty be best placed, next to that which we have all been encouraged to feel in the guardianship and guidance of that Almighty Being whose power regulates the destiny of nations.

Saturday, March 4, 1809, in his First Inaugural Address.[13]

4th
President of the
United States
(1809-1817)

James
Madison
(1751-1836)

I do therefore recommend the third Thursday of August next, as a convenient day, to be set apart for the devout purpose of rendering the Sovereign of the Universe and the Benefactor of mankind the public homage due to His holy attributes.

Thursday, July 9, 1812, in a Proclamation of a National Day of Public Humiliation and Prayer.[14]

) should be compelled to shrink if I had less reliance on the support of an enlightened and generous people, and felt less deeply a conviction that the war with a powerful nation, which forms so prominent a feature in our situation, is stamped with that justice which invites the smiles of Heaven on the means of conducting it to a successful termination. Thursday, March 4, 1813, in his Second Inaugural Address.[15]

4th
President of the
United States
(1809-1817)

James
Madison
(1751-1836)

4th
President of the
United States
(1809-1817)

James
Madison
(1751-1836)

To the same Almighty Power that He would look down with compassion on our infirmities; that He would pardon our manifold transgressions and awaken and strengthen in all the wholesome purposes of repentance.

Friday, July 23, 1813, in a Proclamation of a National Day of Public Humiliation and Prayer.[16]

I enter on the trust to which I have been called by the suffrages of my fellow-citizens with my fervent prayers to the Almighty that He will be graciously pleased to continue to us that protection which He has already so conspicuously displayed.

Tuesday, March 4, 1817, in his First Inaugural Address.[17]

5th
President of the
United States
(1817-1825)

James
Monroe
(1758-1831)

5th
President of the
United States
(1817-1825)

James
Monroe
(1758-1831)

*O*ur most excellent system of government, the powerful instrument in the hands of our All-Merciful Creator in securing to us these blessings.

Tuesday, November 14, 1820, in his Fourth Annual Message to Congress.[18]

℃he liberty, prosperity, and happiness of our country will always be the object of my most fervent prayers to the Supreme Author of All Good.

Monday, March 5, 1821, in his Second Inaugural Address.[19]

or these blessings we owe to Almighty God, from whom we derive them, and with profound reverence, our most grateful and unceasing acknowledgments.

Tuesday, December 7, 1824, in his Eighth Annual Message to Congress.[20]

K nowing that "Except the Lord keep the city, the watchman waketh in vain," with fervent supplications for His favor, to His overruling providence I commit with humble but fearless confidence my own fate and the future destinies of my country.

Friday, March 4, 1825, in his Inaugural Address.[21]

23

6th
President of the
United States
(1825-1829)

John Quincy
Adams
(1767-1848)

There has, indeed, rarely been a period in the history of civilized man in which the general condition of the Christian nations has been marked so extensively by peace and prosperity.

Tuesday, December 6, 1825, in his First Annual Message to Congress.[22]

May we not humbly hope that to them too it was a pledge of transition from gloom to glory, and that while their mortal vestments were sinking into the clod of the valley their emancipated spirits were ascending to the bosom of their God!

Tuesday, December 5, 1826, in his Second Annual Message to Congress, commenting on the death of Thomas Jefferson and John Adams.[23]

6th
President of the
United States
(1825-1829)

John Quincy
Adams
(1767-1848)

Savages, whom it was our policy and our duty to use our influence in converting to Christianity and in bringing within the pale of civilization....We have had the rare good fortune of teaching them the arts of civilization and the doctrines of Christianity.

Tuesday, December 2, 1828, in his Fourth Annual Message to Congress.[24]

A firm reliance on the goodness of that Power whose providence mercifully protected our national infancy, and has since upheld our liberties.

Wednesday, March 4, 1829, in his First Inaugural Address, less than three months after his beloved wife died.[25]

7th
President of the
United States
(1829-1837)

Andrew
Jackson
(1767-1845)

27

7th
President of the
United States
(1829-1837)

Andrew
Jackson
(1767-1845)

According to the terms of an agreement between the United States and the United Society of Christian Indians the latter have a claim to an annuity of $400.

Wednesday, January 20, 1830, in a message to Congress.[26]

It is my fervent prayer to that Almighty Being before whom I now stand, and who has kept us in His hands from the infancy of our Republic to the present day.

Monday, March 4, 1833, in his Second Inaugural Address.[27]

7th
President of the
United States
(1829-1837)

Andrew
Jackson
(1767-1845)

7th
President of the
United States
(1829-1837)

Andrew
Jackson
(1767-1845)

If the Almighty Being who has hitherto sustained and protected me will but vouchsafe to make my feeble powers instrumental to such a result, I shall anticipate with pleasure the place to be assigned me in the history of my country.

Tuesday, April 15, 1834, in a Protest message to the United States Senate.[28]

) only look to the gracious protection of that Divine Being whose strengthening support I humbly solicit, and whom I fervently pray to look down upon us all.

Saturday, March 4, 1837, in his Inaugural Address.[29]

8th
President of the
United States
(1837-1841)

Martin Van
Buren
(1782-1862)

*W*e can only feel more deeply the responsibility of the respective trusts that have been confided to us, and under the pressure of difficulties unite in invoking the guidance and aid of the Supreme Ruler of Nations.

Monday, September 4, 1837, in a Special Session Message to Congress.[30]

*G*eneral prosperity which has been heretofore so bountifully bestowed upon us by the Author of All Good still continues to call for our warmest gratitude.

Monday, December 2, 1839, in his Third Annual Message to Congress.[31]

8th
President of the
United States
(1837-1841)

Martin Van
Buren
(1782-1862)

8th
President of the
United States
(1837-1841)

Martin Van
Buren
(1782-1862)

Our devout gratitude is due to the Supreme Being for having graciously continued to our beloved country through the vicissitudes of another year the invaluable blessings.
Saturday, December 5, 1840, in his Fourth Annual Message to Congress.[32]

We admit of no government by divine right, believing that so far as power is concerned the Beneficent Creator has made no distinction amongst men.

Thursday, March 4, 1841, in his Inaugural Address, delivered only 30 days before his death.[33]

9th
President of the
United States
(1841-1841)

William Henry
Harrison
(1773-1841)

35

9th
President of the
United States
(1841-1841)

William Henry
Harrison
(1773-1841)

he maxim which our ancestors derived from the mother country that "freedom of the press is the great bulwark of civil and religious liberty" is one of the most precious legacies which they have left us.

Thursday, March 4, 1841, in his Inaugural Address, delivered only 30 days before his death.[34]

The tendencies of all such governments in their decline is to monarchy, and the antagonist principle to liberty there is the spirit of faction - a spirit which assumes the character and in times of great excitement imposes itself upon the people as the genuine spirit of freedom, and, like the false christs whose coming was foretold by the Savior, seeks to, and were it possible would, impose upon the true and most faithful disciples of liberty.

March 4, 1841, in his Inaugural Address, delivered only 30 days before his death.[35]

William Henry
Harrison
(1773-1841)

I deem the present occasion sufficiently important and solemn to justify me in expressing to my fellow citizens a profound reverence for the Christian religion, and a thorough conviction that sound morals, religious liberty, and a just sense of religious responsibility are essentially connected with all true and lasting happiness.

Thursday, March 4, 1841, in his Inaugural Address, delivered only 30 days before his death.[36]

My earnest prayer shall be constantly addressed to the All-Wise and All-Powerful Being who made me, and by whose dispensation I am called to the high office of President.

Friday, April 9, 1841, in his Inaugural Address delivered upon assuming the Presidency after the death of President Harrison.[37]

10th
President of the
United States
(1841-1845)

John
Tyler
(1790-1862)

10th
President of the
United States
(1841-1845)

John
Tyler
(1790-1862)

***W**hen a Christian people feel themselves to be overtaken by a great public calamity, it becomes them to humble themselves under the dispensation of Divine Providence.*

Tuesday, April 13, 1841, in a Proclamation of a National Day of Fasting and Prayer, issued upon assuming the Presidency after the death of President Harrison.[38]

We have continued reason to express our profound gratitude to the Great Creator of All Things for the numberless benefits conferred upon us as a people.

Tuesday, December 6, 1842, in his Second Annual Message to the Senate and House of Representatives.[39]

10th
President of the
United States
(1841-1845)

John
Tyler
(1790-1862)

*O*ur *prayers should evermore be offered up to the Father of the Universe for His wisdom to direct us in the path of our duty so as to enable us to consummate these high purposes.*
Tuesday, December 3, 1844, in his Fourth Annual Message to Congress.[40]

I fervently invoke the aid of that Almighty Ruler of the Universe in whose hands are the destinies of nations and of men to guard this Heaven-favored land against the mischiefs which without His guidance might arise from an unwise public policy.

Tuesday, March 4, 1845, in his Inaugural Address.[41]

11th
President of the
United States
(1845-1849)

James Knox
Polk
(1795-1849)

T hrice happy in death, for while he believed the liberties of his country imperishable and was cheered by visions of its constant advancement, he departed from this life in a full hope of a blessed immortality through the merits and atonement of the Redeemer.

Monday, June 16, 1845, upon the death of Andrew Jackson, in General Order No. 27 to Acting Secretary of War and Secretary of the Navy, George Bancroft.[42]

*I*t becomes us in humility to make our devout acknowledgements to the Supreme Ruler of the Universe for the inestimable civil and religious blessings with which we are favored.

Tuesday, December 2, 1845, in his First Annual Message to Congress.[43]

11th
President of the
United States
(1845-1849)

James Knox
Polk
(1795-1849)

No country has been so much favored, or should acknowledge with deeper reverence the manifestations of Divine protection. An all-wise Creator directed and guarded us in our infant struggle for freedom and has constantly watched over our surprising progress. Tuesday, December 7, 1847, in his Third Annual Message to Congress.[44]

I congratulate you, my fellow-citizens, upon the high state of prosperity to which the goodness of Divine Providence has conducted our common country. Let us invoke a continuance of the same protecting care which has led us from small beginnings to the eminence we this day occupy.

Monday, March 5, 1849, in his Inaugural Address, which he delivered a day later than usual, refusing to be sworn in on Sunday in honor of the Sabbath.[45]

Zachary
Taylor
(1784-1850)

It is fitting that a people whose reliance has ever been in His protection should humble themselves before His throne, and, while acknowledging past transgressions, ask a continuance of the Divine mercy.

Tuesday, July 3, 1849, in a Proclamation of a National Day of Prayer during an epidemic of cholera.[46]

𝒯he only ground of hope for the continuance of our free institutions is in the proper moral and religious training of the children.

Wednesday, July 4, 1849, in an address delivered at a Sabbath-school celebration in the city of Washington.[47]

12th
President of the
United States
(1849-1850)

Zachary
Taylor
(1784-1850)

49

12th
President of the
United States
(1849-1850)

Zachary
Taylor
(1784-1850)

he Almighty has at length deigned to stay His hand and to restore the inestimable blessing of general health to a people who acknowledged His power, deprecated His wrath, and implored His merciful protection.

Tuesday, December 4, 1849, in his First Annual Message to Congress.[48]

rely upon Him who holds in His hands the destinies of nations to endow me with the requisite strength for the task and to avert from our country the evils apprehended from the heavy calamity which has befallen us.

Wednesday, July 10, 1850, in an address to Congress, delivered upon assuming the Presidency after the death of President Taylor.[49]

13th
President of the
United States
(1850-1853)

Millard
Fillmore
(1800-1874)

13th
President of the
United States
(1850-1853)

Millard
Fillmore
(1800-1874)

I can not bring this communication to a close without invoking you to join me in humble and devout thanks to the Great Ruler of Nations for the multiplied blessings which He has graciously bestowed upon us.

Monday, December 2, 1850, in his First Annual Message to Congress.[50]

*A*t the same time....we must be impressed with a grateful sense of our profound obligations to a beneficent Providence, whose paternal care is so manifest in the happiness of this highly favored land.

Tuesday, December 2, 1851, in his Second Annual Message to Congress.[51]

13th
President of the
United States
(1850-1853)

Millard
Fillmore
(1800-1874)

Our grateful thanks are due to an all-merciful Providence, not only for staying the pestilence which in different forms has desolated some of our cities, but for crowning the labors of the husbandman with an abundant harvest.

Monday, December 6, 1852, in his Third Annual Message to Congress.[52]

It must be felt that there is no national security but in the Nation's humble, acknowledged dependence upon God and His overruling providence.
Friday, March 4, 1853, in his Inaugural Address [53]

14th
President of the
United States
(1853-1857)

Franklin
Pierce
(1804-1869)

*O*urs is almost, if not absolutely, the solitary power of Christendom having a surplus revenue drawn immediately from imposts on commerce.

Monday, December 5, 1853, in his First Annual Message to Congress.[54]

*T*o harmonize a sincere and ardent devotion to the institutions of religious faith with the most universal religious toleration....whilst exalting the condition of the Republic, to assure to it the legitimate influence and the benign authority of a great example amongst all the powers of Christendom.

Monday, December 4, 1854, in his Second Annual Message.[55]

14th
President of the
United States
(1853-1857)

Franklin
Pierce
(1804-1869)

I communicate to the Senate herewith…a treaty made and concluded at Fort Leavenworth, Kansas Territory, on the 16th day of December, 1856, between Indian Agent Benjamin F. Robinson, commissioner on the part of the United States, the principal men of the Christian Indians, and Gottleib F. Oehler, on behalf of the board of elders of the northern diocese of the Church of the United Brethren.

Friday, January 16, 1857, in a message to the United States Senate.[56]

We *ought to cultivate peace,*
commerce, and friendship with
all nations, and this not merely as the
best means of promoting our own
material interests, but in a spirit of
Christian benevolence toward our fellow-
men, wherever their lot may be cast.
Wednesday, March 4, 1857, in his Inaugural Address.[57]

15th
President of the
United States
(1857-1861)

James
Buchanan
(1791-1868)

15th
President of the
United States
(1857-1861)

James
Buchanan
(1791-1868)

We are obliged as a Christian and moral nation to consider what would be the effect upon unhappy Africa itself if we should reopen the slave trade....When a market for African slaves shall no longer be furnished in Cuba, and thus all the world be closed against this trade, we may then indulge a reasonable hope for the gradual improvement of Africa.

Monday, December 19, 1859, in his Third Annual Message to Congress.[58]

) t is with great satisfaction I communicate the fact that since the date of my last annual message not a single slave has been imported into the United States....It surely ought to be the prayer of every Christian and patriot that such expeditions may never again receive countenance in our country or depart from our shores.

Monday, December 3, 1860, in his Fourth Annual Message to Congress.[59]

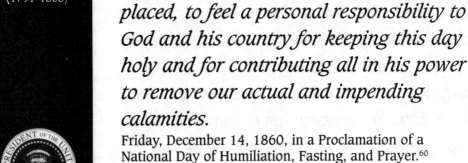

15th
President of the
United States
(1857-1861)

James
Buchanan
(1791-1868)

et me invoke every individual, in whatever sphere of life he may be placed, to feel a personal responsibility to God and his country for keeping this day holy and for contributing all in his power to remove our actual and impending calamities.

Friday, December 14, 1860, in a Proclamation of a National Day of Humiliation, Fasting, and Prayer.[60]

Intelligence, patriotism, Christianity, and a firm reliance on Him who has never yet forsaken this favored land, are still competent to adjust in the best way all our present difficulty.

Monday, March 4, 1861, in his First Inaugural Address.[61]

16th
President of the
United States
(1861-1865)

Abraham
Lincoln
(1809-1865)

Abraham
Lincoln
(1809-1865)

*I*t is fit and becoming in all people, at all times, to acknowledge and revere the Supreme Government of God; to bow in humble submission to His chastisement; to confess and deplore their sins and transgressions in the full conviction that "the fear of the Lord is the beginning of wisdom."

Monday, August 12, 1861, in a Proclamation of a National Day of Humiliation, Prayer, and Fasting, issued after the Union defeat at the *Battle of Bull Run*.[62]

We have forgotten God. We have forgotten the gracious Hand which preserved us in peace, and multiplied and enriched and strengthened us; and we have vainly imagined, in the deceitfulness of our hearts, that all these blessings were produced by some superior wisdom and virtue of our own. Intoxicated with unbroken success, we have become too self-sufficient to feel the necessity of redeeming and preserving grace, too proud to pray to the God that made us!

Monday, March 30, 1863, in a Proclamation of a National Day of Humiliation, Fasting and Prayer.[63]

16th
President of the
United States
(1861-1865)

Abraham
Lincoln
(1809-1865)

Yet, if God will that it continue until all the wealth piled by the bondsmen's two hundred and fifty years of unrequited toil shall be sunk, and until every drop of blood drawn with the lash shall be paid by another drawn with the sword, as was said three thousand years ago, so still it must be said "the judgements of the Lord are true and righteous altogether."

Saturday, March 4, 1865, in his Second Inaugural Address, just 45 days before his assassination.[64]

) recommend my fellow-citizens then to assemble in their respective places of worship, there to unite in solemn service to Almighty God in memory of the good man who has been removed, so that all shall be occupied at the same time in contemplation of his virtues and in sorrow for his sudden and violent end.

Tuesday, April 25, 1865, in a Proclamation of a National Day of Humiliation and Mourning, issued upon assuming the Presidency after the death of President Lincoln.[65]

17th
President of the
United States
(1865-1869)

Andrew
Johnson
(1808-1875)

17th
President of the
United States
(1865-1869)

Andrew
Johnson
(1808-1875)

I n offering these national thanksgivings, praises, and supplications we have the divine assurance that "the Lord remaineth a king forever; them that are meek shall He guide in judgement and such as are gentle shall He learn His way; the Lord shall give strength to His people, and the Lord shall give to His people the blessing of peace."

Monday, October 8, 1866, Proclamation of a National Day of Thanksgiving and Praise.[66]

), ____ ____, do solemnly swear (or affirm), in presence of Almighty God, that I will henceforth faithfully support, protect, and defend the Constitution of the United States and the Union of the States thereunder, and that I will in like manner abide by and faithfully support all laws and proclamations which have been made during the late rebellion with reference to the emancipation of slaves. So help me God.

Saturday, September 7, 1867, oath prescribed in the Proclamation of Amnesty and Pardon to the participants of the Confederate insurrection.[67]

17th
President of the
United States
(1865-1869)

Andrew
Johnson
(1808-1875)

17th
President of the
United States
(1865-1869)

Andrew
Johnson
(1808-1875)

The restoration of the States to their proper legal relations with the Federal Government...would be the greatest temporal blessing which God, in His kindest Providence, could bestow upon this nation....Christianity and civilization have made such progress that recourse to a punishment so cruel and unjust would meet with condemnation of all unprejudiced and right-minded men.
Tuesday, December 3, 1867, in his Third Annual Message to Congress.[68]

ask patient forbearance one toward another throughout the land, and a determined effort on the part of every citizen to do his share toward cementing a happy union; and I ask the prayers of the nation to Almighty God in behalf of this consummation.

Thursday, March 4, 1869, in his First Inaugural Address.[69]

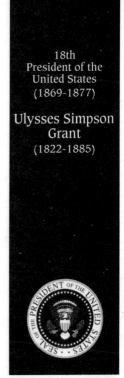

Ulysses Simpson
Grant
(1822-1885)

18th
President of the
United States
(1869-1877)

Ulysses Simpson
Grant
(1822-1885)

The societies selected are allowed to name their own agents, subject to the approval of the Executive, and are expected to watch over them and aid them as missionaries, to Christianize and civilize the Indians, and to train him in the arts of peace.

Monday, December 5, 1870, in his Second Annual Message to Congress.[70]

I do believe that our Great Maker is preparing the world, in His own good time, to become one nation, speaking one language, and then armies and navies will no longer be required.

Tuesday, March 4, 1873, in his Second Inaugural Address.[71]

18th
President of the
United States
(1869-1877)

Ulysses Simpson
Grant
(1822-1885)

We should not forget the source from whence they are derived and the extent of our obligation to the Father of All Mercies. We have full reason to renew our thanks to Almighty God....By His continuing mercy civil and religious liberty have been maintained.
Wednesday, October 27, 1875, in a Proclamation of a National Day of Thanksgiving.[72]

*L**ooking for the guidance of that Divine Hand by which the destinies of nations and individuals are shaped, I call upon you, Senators, Representatives, judges, fellow-citizens, here and everywhere, to unite with me in an earnest effort to secure to our country the blessings.*

Monday, March 5, 1877, in his Inaugural Address, which he delivered a day later than usual, refusing to be sworn in on Sunday in honor of the Sabbath.[73]

19th
President of the
United States
(1877-1881)

Rutherford
Bichard Hayes
(1822-1893)

SEAL OF THE PRESIDENT OF THE UNITED STATES

19th
President of the
United States
(1877-1881)

Rutherford
Bichard Hayes
(1822-1893)

The Government of the Samoan Islands..., having made considerable progress in Christian civilization and the development of trade, are doubtful of their ability to maintain peace and independence without the aid of some stronger power.
Monday, December 3, 1877, in his First Annual Message.[74]

I earnestly recommend that, withdrawing themselves from secular cares and labors, the people of the United States do meet together on that day in their respective places of worship, there to give thanks and praise to Almighty God for His mercies and to devoutly beseech their continuance.

Monday, November 3, 1879, in a Proclamation of a National Day of Thanksgiving and Prayer.[75]

19th
President of the
United States
(1877-1881)

Rutherford
Bichard Hayes
(1822-1893)

19th
President of the
United States
(1877-1881)

Rutherford
Bichard Hayes
(1822-1893)

*A*t no period in their history since the United States became a nation has this people had so abundant and universal reasons for joy and gratitude at the favor of Almighty God or been subject to so profound an obligation to give thanks for His loving kindness and humbly to implore His continued care and protection.

Monday, November 1, 1880, in a Proclamation of a National Day of Thanksgiving.[76]

Fifty years hence our children will not be divided in their opinions concerning our controversies. They will surely bless their fathers and their fathers' God that the Union was preserved, that slavery was overthrown, and that both races were made equal before the law.

Friday, March 4, 1881, in his Inaugural Address.[77]

20th
President of the
United States
(1881-1881)

James Abram
Garfield
(1831-1881)

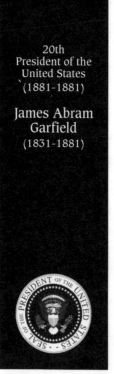

20th
President of the
United States
(1881-1881)

James Abram
Garfield
(1831-1881)

*F*ellow citizens! Clouds and darkness are around Him. His pavilion is dark waters and thick clouds of the skies! Justice and judgment are the establishment of His throne! Mercy and truth shall go before His face. Fellow citizens! God reigns and the Government at Washington still lives!*

Saturday, April 15, 1865, in an address delivered while a U.S. Congressman, after overcoming the shock of President Lincoln's assassination.[78]

If the next centennial does not find us a great nation...it will be because those who represent the enterprise, the culture, and the morality of the nation do not aid in controlling the political forces.

Tuesday, July 4, 1876, in an address commemorating the 100th anniversary of the Declaration of Independence, delivered while serving as the U.S. Congressman chairing the Committee on Appropriations.[79]

20th
President of the
United States
(1881-1881)

James Abram
Garfield
(1831-1881)

20th
President of the
United States
(1881-1881)

James Abram
Garfield
(1831-1881)

*J*ames A. Garfield, President of the United States, died at Elberon, N.J., last night at ten minutes before 11 o'clock. For nearly eighty days he suffered great pain, and during the entire period exhibited extraordinary patience, fortitude, and Christian resignation. Fifty millions of people stand as mourners by his bier.

Saturday, July 2, 1881, after having been in office only 4 months, was shot in the back while in the Washington, D.C., railroad station. He died a few months later on September 19, 1881. The following day, Secretary of State James G. Blaine, writing from Long Branch, N.J., sent this announcement to James Russell Lowell, U.S. Minister in London.[80]

It is fitting that the deep grief which fills all hearts should manifest itself with one accord toward the Throne of Infinite Grace, and that we should bow before the Almighty and seek from Him that consolation in our affliction.

Thursday, September 22, 1881, in a Proclamation of a National Day of Humiliation and Mourning, issued upon assuming the Presidency after the death of President Garfield.[81]

21st
President of the
United States
(1881-1885)

Chester Alan
Arthur
(1829-1886)

21st
President of the
United States
(1881-1885)

Chester Alan
Arthur
(1829-1886)

he countless benefits which have showered upon us during the past twelvemonth call for our fervent gratitude and make it fitting that we should rejoice with thankfulness that the Lord in His infinite mercy has most signally favored our country and our people.

Friday, November 4, 1881, in a Proclamation of a National Day of Thanksgiving and Prayer.[82]

*R*elations with Russia should be strengthened by proper engagements assuring to peaceable Americans who visit the Empire the consideration which is due to them as citizens of a friendly state. This is especially needful with respect to American Israelites, whose classification with the native Hebrew has evoked energetic remonstrances.

Tuesday, December 6, 1881, in his First Annual Message to Congress.[83]

21st
President of the
United States
(1881-1885)

Chester Alan
Arthur
(1829-1886)

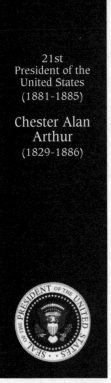

21st
President of the
United States
(1881-1885)

Chester Alan
Arthur
(1829-1886)

I do therefore recommend that on the day above appointed the people rest from their accustomed labors and, meeting in their several places of worship, express their devout gratitude to God that He hath dealt so bountifully with this Nation and pray that His grace and favor abide with it forever.

Friday, October 26, 1883, in a Proclamation of a National Day of Thanksgiving.[84]

*A*nd let us not trust to human effort alone, but humbly acknowledge the power and goodness of Almighty God who presides over the destiny of nations, and who has at all times been revealed in our country's history, let us invoke His aid and His blessings upon our labors.

Wednesday, March 4, 1885, in his First Inaugural Address.[85]

22nd President of the United States (1885-1889)

(Stephen) Grover Cleveland (1837-1908)

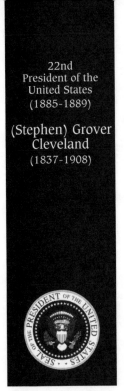

22nd
President of the
United States
(1885-1889)

(Stephen) Grover
Cleveland
(1837-1908)

et all secular business be suspended, and let the people assemble in their usual places of worship and with prayer and songs of praise devoutly testify their gratitude to the Giver of Every Good and Perfect Gift for all that He has done for us.
Monday, November 2, 1885, in a Proclamation of a National Day of Thanksgiving and Prayer.[86]

The mothers of our land, who rule the Nation as they mold the characters and guide the actions of their sons, live according to God's Holy Ordinances, and each, secure and happy in the exclusive love of the father of her children, sheds the warm light of true womanhood, unperverted and unpolluted, upon all within her pure and wholesome family circle.

Tuesday, December 8, 1885, in his First Annual Message to Congress.[87]

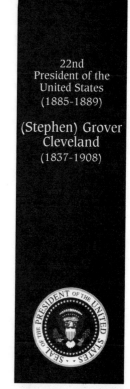

22nd
President of the
United States
(1885-1889)

(Stephen) Grover
Cleveland
(1837-1908)

89

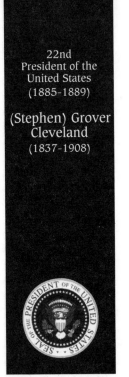

22nd
President of the
United States
(1885-1889)

(Stephen) Grover
Cleveland
(1837-1908)

As we return thanks for all the blessings which we have received from the hand of our Heavenly Father, let us not forget that He has enjoined upon us charity; and on this day of thanksgiving let us generously remember the poor and needy, so that our tribute of praise and gratitude may be acceptable in the sight of the Lord.

Thursday, November 1, 1888, in a Proclamation of a National Day of Thanksgiving and Prayer.[88]

Entering thus solemnly into covenant with each other, we may reverently invoke and confidently extend the favor and help of Almighty God - that He will give to me wisdom, strength, and fidelity, and to our people a spirit of fraternity and a love of righteousness and peace.
Monday, March 4, 1889, in his Inaugural Address.[89]

That the joy of the occasion may be associated with a deep thankfulness in the minds of the people for all our blessings in the past and a devout supplication to God for their gracious continuance in the future, the representatives of the religious creeds, both Christian and Hebrew, have memorialized the Government to designate an hour for prayer and thanksgiving.

Thursday, April 4, 1889, in a Proclamation of a National Day of Prayer and Thanksgiving on the Centennial of Washington's Inauguration.[90]

In November, 1862, President Lincoln quoted the words of Washington to sustain his own views, and announced in a general order that - "...The importance for man and beast of the prescribed weekly rest, the sacred rights of Christian soldiers and sailors, a becoming deference to the best sentiment of a Christian people, and a due regard for the divine will demand that Sunday labor in the Army and Navy be reduced to the measure of strict necessity."

Friday, June 7, 1889, in a General Order issued from the Executive Mansion.[91]

23rd
President of the
United States
(1889-1893)

Benjamin
Harrison
(1833-1901)

Benjamin
Harrison
(1833-1901)

This Government has found occasion to express in a friendly spirit, but with much earnestness, to the Government of the Czar its serious concern because of the harsh measures now being enforced against the Hebrews in Russia. By the revival of antisemitic laws, long in abeyance, great numbers of those unfortunate people have been constrained to abandon their homes and leave the Empire by reason of the impossibility of finding subsistence.
Wednesday, December 9, 1891, in his Third Annual Message.[92]

*A*bove all, I know there is a Supreme *Being who rules the affairs of men and whose goodness and mercy have always followed the American people, and I know He will not turn from us now if we humbly and reverently seek His powerful aid.*

Saturday, March 4, 1893, in his Second Inaugural Address.[93]

24th
President of the
United States
(1893-1897)

(Stephen) Grover
Cleveland
(1837-1908)

The American people should gratefully render thanksgiving and praise to the Supreme Ruler of the Universe....They should also with humility and faith supplicate the Father of All Mercies for continued blessings according to their needs, and they should by deeds of charity seek the favor of the Giver of Every Good and Perfect Gift.

Thursday, November 1, 1894, in a Proclamation of a National Day of Thanksgiving and Prayer.[94]

eported massacres of Christians in Armenia and the development there and in other districts of a spirit of fanatic hostility to Christian influences naturally excited apprehension for the safety of the devoted men and women who, as dependents of the foreign missionary societies in the United States, reside in Turkey....No efforts have been spared in their behalf.

Monday, December 2, 1895, in his Third Annual Message to Congress.[95]

24th
President of the
United States
(1893-1897)

(Stephen) Grover
Cleveland
(1837-1908)

24th
President of the
United States
(1893-1897)

(Stephen) Grover
Cleveland
(1837-1908)

loody butchery of men, women, and children, made martyrs to their profession of Christian faith....I do not believe that the present somber prospect in Turkey will be long permitted .... It so mars the humane and enlightened civilization that belongs to the close of the nineteenth century that it seems hardly possible that the earnest demand of good people throughout the Christian world for its corrective treatment will remain unanswered.

Monday, December 7, 1896, in his Eighth Annual Message.[96]

I assume the arduous and responsible duties of President of the United States, relying upon the support of my countrymen and invoking the guidance of Almighty God. Our faith teaches that there is no safer reliance than upon the God of our fathers, who has so singularly favored the American people in every national trial, and who will not forsake us so long as we obey His commandments and walk humbly in His footsteps.

Thursday, March 4, 1897, in his First Inaugural Address.[97]

25th
President of the
United States
(1897-1901)

William
McKinley
(1843-1901)

25th
President of the
United States
(1897-1901)

William
McKinley
(1843-1901)

𝒯he abhorrent conditions which have existed for more than three years in the island of Cuba, so near our own borders, have shocked the moral sense of the people of the United States, have been a disgrace to Christian civilization, culminating, as they have, in the destruction of a United States battle ship [U.S.S. Maine], with 266 of its officers and crew, while on a friendly visit in the harbor of Havana.

Wednesday, April 20, 1898, approving a Joint Resolution of Congress.[98]

It has pleased the Almighty God to bring our nation in safety and honor through another year....We have been generally exempt from pestilence and other great calamities; and even the tragic visitation which overwhelmed the city of Galveston made evident the sentiments of sympathy and Christian charity by virtue of which we are one united people.

Monday, October 29, 1900, in a Proclamation of a National Day of Thanksgiving and Praise.[99]

25th
President of the
United States
(1897-1901)

William
McKinley
(1843-1901)

25th
President of the
United States
(1897-1901)

William
McKinley
(1843-1901)

I enter upon its administration appreciating the great responsibilities which attach to this renewed honor and commission, promising unreserved devotion on my part to their faithful discharge and reverently invoking for my guidance the direction and favor of Almighty God. Monday, March 4, 1901, in his Second Inaugural Address.[100]

President McKinley crowned a life of largest love for his fellow men, of earnest endeavor for their welfare, by a death of Christian fortitude; and both the way in which he lived his life and the way in which, in the supreme hour of trial, he met death will remain forever a precious heritage of our people.

Saturday, September 14, 1901, in a Proclamation of a National Day of Mourning and Prayer, issued upon assuming the Presidency after the death of President McKinley.[101]

26th
President of the
United States
(1901-1909)

Theodore
Roosevelt
(1858-1919)

Theodore
Roosevelt
(1858-1919)

I ...do recommend that on that day they cease from their ordinary occupations and gather in their several places of worship or in their homes, devoutly to give thanks unto Almighty God for the benefits he has conferred upon us as individuals and as a nation, and to beseech Him that in the future His Divine favor may be continued to us.

Tuesday, November 1, 1904, in a Proclamation of a National Day of Thanksgiving.[102]

It has proved very difficult to secure from Russia the right for our Jewish fellow-citizens to receive passports .... Such conduct is not only unjust and irritating toward us, but it is difficult to see its wisdom from Russia's standpoint....If an American Jew or an American Christian misbehaves himself in Russia he can at once be driven out; but the ordinary American Jew, like the ordinary American Christian, would behave just about as he behaves here.

Tuesday, December 6, 1904, in his Fourth Annual Message to Congress.[103]

26th President of the United States (1901-1909)

Theodore Roosevelt (1858-1919)

26th
President of the
United States
(1901-1909)

Theodore
Roosevelt
(1858-1919)

No people on earth have more cause to be thankful than ours, and this is said reverently, in no spirit of boastfulness in our own strength, but with gratitude to the Giver of Good who has blessed us....If we fail, the cause of free self-government throughout the world will rock to its foundations.

Saturday, March 4, 1905, in his Inaugural Address.[104]

I invoke the considerate sympathy and support of my fellow-citizens and the aid of the Almighty God in the discharge of my responsible duties.

Thursday, March 4, 1909, in his Inaugural Address.[105]

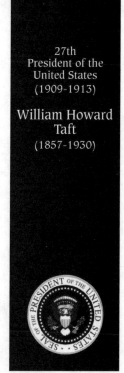

27th
President of the
United States
(1909-1913)

William Howard
Taft
(1857-1930)

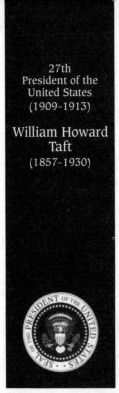

A God-fearing nation, like ours, owes it to its inborn and sincere sense of moral duty to testify its devout gratitude to the All-Giver for the countless benefits its has enjoyed. For many years it has been customary at the close of the year for the national Executive to call upon his fellow countrymen to offer praise and thanks to God for the manifold blessings vouchsafed to them.

Thursday, November 7, 1912, in a Proclamation of a National Day of Thanksgiving.[106]

It is altogether fitting that we should humbly and gratefully acknowledge the Divine Source of these blessings. Therefore, I hereby appoint...a day of general thanksgiving, and I call upon the people on that day, laying aside their usual vocations, to repair to their churches and unite in appropriate services of praise and thanks to Almighty God.

Monday, November 15, 1909, in a Proclamation of a National Day of Thanksgiving.[107]

27th President of the United States (1909-1913)

William Howard Taft (1857-1930)

27th
President of the
United States
(1909-1913)

William Howard
Taft
(1857-1930)

O *ur defense of the Panama Canal, together with our enormous world trade and our missionary outposts on the frontiers of civilization, require us to recognize our position as one of the foremost in the family of nations, and to clothe ourselves with sufficient naval power to give force to our reasonable demands, and to give weight to our influence in those directions of progress that a powerful Christian nation should advocate.*

Friday, December 6, 1912, in his Annual Message to Congress, part II.[108]

Men's hearts wait upon us; men's lives hang in the balance; men's hopes call upon us today what we will do. Who shall live up to the great trust? Who dare fail to try? I summon all honest men, all patriotic, all forward-looking men to my side. God helping me, I will not fail them.

March 4, 1913, in his First Inaugural Address.[109]

28th
President of the
United States
(1913-1921)

(Thomas)
Woodrow Wilson
(1856-1924)

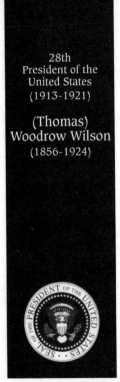

In their ardent heat we shall, in God's Providence, let us hope, be purged of faction and division....I know now what the task means. I realize to the full the responsibility which it involves. I pray God I may be given the wisdom and the prudence to do my duty in the true spirit of this great people.

Monday, March 5, 1917, in his Second Inaugural Address.[110]

The President...enjoins the orderly observance of the Sabbath by the officers and men in the military and naval service of the United States. The importance for man and beast of the prescribed weekly rest, the sacred rights of Christian soldiers and sailors, a becoming deference to the best sentiment of a Christian people, and a due regard for the Divine Will demand that Sunday labor in the Army and Navy be reduced to the measure of strict necessity.

Sunday, January 20, 1918, in an Executive Order to the Army and Navy enjoining Sabbath observance.[111]

28th
President of the
United States
(1913-1921)

(Thomas)
Woodrow Wilson
(1856-1924)

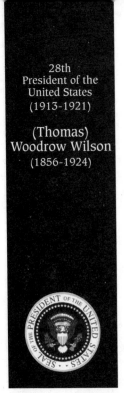

The Senate Committee on Foreign Relations has clearly established the truth of the reported massacres and other atrocities from which the Armenian people have suffered....The sympathy for Armenia among our people has sprung from untainted consciences, pure Christian faith and an earnest desire to see Christian people everywhere succored in their time of suffering.

Monday, May 24, 1920, in a special message to Congress asking permission to assume the mandate for Armenia under the League of Nations.[112]

)accept my part...and implore the favor and guidance of God in His Heaven. With these I am unafraid, and confidently face the future. I have taken the solemn oath of office on that passage of Holy Writ wherein it is asked: "What doth the Lord require of thee but to do justly, and to love mercy, and to walk humbly with thy God." This I plight to God and country.

Friday, March 4, 1921, in his Inaugural Address.[113]

29th
President of the
United States
(1921-1923)

Warren Gamaliel
Harding
(1865-1923)

In the death gloom of gas, the bursting of shells and rain of bullets, men face more intimately the great God over all....I can sense the prayers of our people...that this Armistice Day shall mark the beginning of a new and lasting era of peace on earth, good will among men. Let me join in that prayer. Our Father who are in heaven, hallowed be Thy name. Thy kingdom come, Thy will be done on earth, as it is in heaven. Give us this day ....Amen.

Friday, November 11, 1921, burying an Unknown Soldier in Arlington Cemetery.[114]

shall call upon your patriotism. I shall beseech your humanity. I shall invoke your Christianity. I shall reach to the very depths of your love for you fellow men of whatever race or creed throughout the world. I shall speak, as I speak now, with all the earnestness and power of the sincerity that is in me and in perfect faith that God will keep clear and receptive your understanding. I could not do otherwise. My soul yearns for peace.

Thursday, June 21, 1923, in his address on the International Court of Justice, delivered in St. Louis, Missouri.[115]

Warren Gamaliel
Harding
(1865-1923)

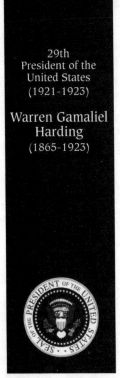

29th
President of the
United States
(1921-1923)

Warren Gamaliel
Harding
(1865-1923)

I thank you from my heart for permitting me to participate in doing homage to those brave souls. I rejoice particularly in the opportunity afforded me of voicing my appreciation both as President of the United States and as one who honestly tries to be a Christian soldier, of the signal service of the martyred Whitman.

Tuesday, July 3, 1923, just one month before his death, in a speech in Meacham, Oregon.[116]

I earnestly recommend the people to assemble on that day in their respective places of divine worship, there to bow down in submission to the will of Almighty God, and to pay out of full hearts the homage of love and reverence to the memory of the great and good President, whose death has so sorely smitten the Nation.

Saturday, August 4, 1923, in a Proclamation of a National Day of Mourning and Prayer issued upon assuming the Presidency after the death of President Harding.[117]

30th
President of the
United States
(1923-1929)

(John) Calvin
Coolidge
(1872-1933)

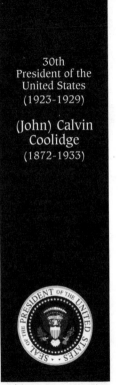

30th
President of the
United States
(1923-1929)

(John) Calvin
Coolidge
(1872-1933)

*A*merica seeks no earthly empires built on blood and force. No ambition, no temptation, lures her to thought of foreign dominions. The legions which she sends forth are armed, not with the sword, but with the Cross. The higher state to which she seeks the allegiance of all mankind is not of human, but Divine origin. She cherishes no purpose save to merit the favor of Almighty God.

Wednesday, March 4, 1925, in his Inaugural Address.[118]

It seems to me perfectly plain that the authority of law, the right to equality, liberty and property, under American institutions, have for their foundation reverence for God. If we could imagine that to be swept away, these institutions of our American government could not long survive....But I know they will continue to stand. We may perish, but they will endure. They are founded on the Rock of Ages.

Sunday, September 21, 1924, in addressing the Holy Name Society, Washington, D.C.[119]

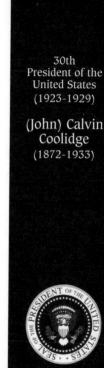

30th
President of the
United States
(1923-1929)

(John) Calvin
Coolidge
(1872-1933)

30th
President of the
United States
(1923-1929)

(John) Calvin
Coolidge
(1872-1933)

Haym Solomon, Polish Jew financier of the Revolution....personally advanced large sums to...patriot leaders who testified that without his aid they could not have carried on....They give due credit to the people among whom the Holy Scriptures came into being.... "Hebraic mortar cemented the foundations of American democracy." ... If American democracy is to remain the greatest hope of humanity, it must continue abundantly in the faith of the Bible.

Sunday, May 3, 1925, laying the cornerstone of the Jewish Community Center, Washington, D.C.[120]

This occasion is...a dedication and consecration under God to the highest office in service of our people....Knowing what the task means and the responsibility which it involves, I beg your tolerance, your aid, and your cooperation. I ask the help of Almighty God in this service to my country to which you have called me.

Monday, March 4, 1929, in his Inaugural Address.[121]

31st
President of the
United States
(1929-1933)

Herbert Clark
Hoover
(1874-1964)

Herbert Clark
Hoover
(1874-1964)

If, by the grace of God, we have passed the worst of this storm, the future months will be easy....If we can maintain this courage and resolution we shall have written this new chapter in national life in terms to which our whole idealism has aspired. May God grant to us the spirit and strength to carry through to the end.

Monday, April 27, 1931, in speaking before the Gridiron Club.[122]

*A*merican life is builded and can alone survive upon the translation into individual action of that fundamental philosophy announced by the Savior nineteen centuries ago. Part of our national suffering today is from failure to observe these primary yet inexorable laws of human relationship. Modern society can not survive with the defense of Cain, "Am I my brother's keeper?"

Sunday, October 18, 1931, in an address which began a nation-wide drive to aid the private relief agencies during the Great Depression.[123]

31st
President of the
United States
(1929-1933)

Herbert Clark
Hoover
(1874-1964)

Herbert Clark
Hoover
(1874-1964)

We maintain the spiritual impulses in our people for generous giving and generous service - in the spirit that each is his brother's keeper....Many a family today is carrying a neighbor family over the trough of this depression not alone with material aid but with that encouragement which maintains courage and faith.

Thursday, September 15, 1932, in an address delivered at the White House to the leaders of the "national drive" committee for voluntary relief agencies.[124]

The only thing we have to fear is fear itself. We face arduous days that lie before us in the warm courage of national unity; with the clear consciousness of seeking old and precious moral values....In this dedication of a nation we humbly ask the blessing of God. May He protect each and every one of us! May He guide me in the days to come.
Saturday, March 4, 1933, in his First Inaugural Address.[125]

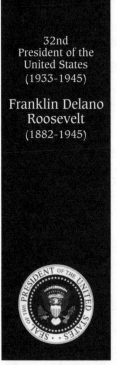

32nd
President of the
United States
(1933-1945)

Franklin Delano
Roosevelt
(1882-1945)

While this duty rests upon me I shall do my utmost to speak their purpose and to do their will, seeking Divine Guidance to help each and every one to give light to them that sit in darkness and to guide our feet into the way of peace.

Wednesday, January 20, 1937, in his Second Inaugural Address.[126]

)f the spirit of America were killed, even though the Nation's body and mind, constricted in an alien world, lived on, the America we know would have perished. That spirit - that faith - speaks to us in our daily lives in ways often unnoticed....We do not retreat. We are not content to stand still. As Americans, we go forward in the service of our country by the will of God.

Monday, January 20, 1941, in his Third Inaugural Address.[127]

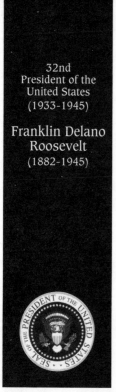

In the presence of God - I know that it is America's purpose that we shall not fail....The Almighty God has blessed our land in many ways. So we pray to Him now for the vision to see our way clearly - to see the way that leads to a better life for ourselves and for all our fellow men - to the achievement of His will, to peace on earth.

Saturday, January 20, 1945, in his Fourth Inaugural Address.[128]

At this moment I have in my heart a prayer. As I have assumed my heavy duties, I humbly pray to Almighty God in the words of King Solomon: "Give therefore Thy servant an understanding heart to judge Thy people that I may discern between good and bad; for who is able to judge this Thy so great a people?" I ask only to be a good and faithful servant of my Lord and my people.

Thursday, April 12, 1945, in his First Address to Congress, delivered upon assuming the Presidency after the death of President Roosevelt.[129]

33rd
President of the
United States
(1945-1953)

Harry S.
Truman
(1884-1972)

131

33rd
President of the
United States
(1945-1953)

Harry S.
Truman
(1884-1972)

In this great country of ours has been demonstrated the fundamental unity of Christianity and democracy.... Whether it be far or near, the kingdom of this world shall become indeed the Kingdom of God and He will reign forever and ever, Lord of Lords and King of Kings. With that message, I wish my countrymen a Merry Christmas and joyous days in the New Year.

Tuesday, December 24, 1946, at the Ceremony lighting the national Christmas tree.[130]

remember well our conversations about the Negeb....I agree fully with your estimate of the importance of the area to Israel, and I deplore any attempt to take it away from Israel. I had thought that my position would have been clear to all the world, particularly in the light of the specific wording of the Democratic Party platform....In closing, I want to tell you how happy and impressed I have been at the remarkable progress made by the new State of Israel.

Monday, November 29, 1948, in a personal letter to Dr. Chaim Weizmann, President of the State of Israel.[131]

33rd
President of the
United States
(1945-1953)

Harry S.
Truman
(1884-1972)

133

33rd
President of the
United States
(1945-1953)

Harry S.
Truman
(1884-1972)

I need the help and the prayers of every one of you....The American people stand firm in the faith which has inspired this Nation from the beginning....We believe that all men are created equal because they are created in the image of God. From this faith we will not be moved....Steadfast in our faith in the Almighty, we will advance toward a world, where man's freedom is secure.

Thursday, January 20, 1949, in his Inaugural Address.[132]

*A*lmighty God, as we stand here at this moment, my future associates in the Executive Branch of government join me in beseeching that Thou will make full and complete our dedication to the service of the people in this throng, and their fellow citizens everywhere. Give us, we pray, the power to discern clearly right from wrong.

Tuesday, January 20, 1953, in his Inaugural Address, the first such address to be televised.[133]

34rd
President of the
United States
(1953-1961)

Dwight David
Eisenhower
(1890-1969)

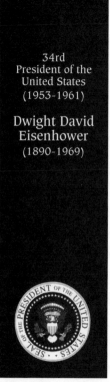

34rd
President of the
United States
(1953-1961)

Dwight David
Eisenhower
(1890-1969)

ach Year the Committee on Religion in American Life reminds us of the importance of faithful church attendance. It urges full support of religious institutions to the end that we may add strength and meaning to the religious virtues - charity, mercy, brotherly love, and faith in Almighty God.

Saturday, October 31, 1953, in a nationally broadcast program for the Committee on Religion in American Life.[134]

*A*ll men are born equal, because each is born in the image of his God. Our whole theory of government finally expressed in our Declaration, you will recall, said... "Man is endowed by his Creator."...Now, any group that binds itself together to awaken all of us to these simple things...is, in my mind, a dedicated, patriotic group that can well take the Bible in one hand and the a flag in the other, and march ahead.

Tuesday, November 9, 1954, addressing the first National Conference on the Spiritual Foundation of American Democracy.[135]

34rd
President of the
United States
(1953-1961)

Dwight David
Eisenhower
(1890-1969)

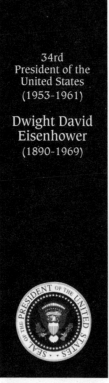

We seek upon our common labor as a nation, the blessings of Almighty God. And the hopes in our hearts fashion the deepest prayers of our whole people....We declare our firm and fixed purpose - the building of a peace with justice in a world where moral law prevails....The prayer of our people carries far beyond our own frontiers, to the wide world.

Monday, January 21, 1957, in his Second Inaugural Address.[136]

The same revolutionary beliefs for which our forebears fought are still at issue around the globe - The belief that the rights of man come not from the generosity of the state but from the hand of God....And so, my fellow Americans - ask not what your country can do for you - ask what you can do for your country....Let us go forth to lead the land we love, asking His blessing and His help, but knowing that here on earth God's work must truly be our own.

Friday, January 20, 1961, in his Inaugural Address.[137]

35rd
President of the
United States
(1961-1963)

John Fitzgerald
Kennedy
(1917-1963)

This nation was then torn by war. This territory had only the simplest elements of civilization....But a university was one of their earliest thoughts, and they summed it up in the motto that they adopted: "Let there be light." What more can be said today regarding all the dark and tangled problems we face than: Let there be light.

Thursday, November 16, 1961, in an address given at the University of Washington.[138]

It ought to be possible, in short, for every American to enjoy the privileges of being American without regard to his race or his color....We are confronted primarily with a moral issue. It is as old as the Scriptures and is as clear as the American Constitution....We face, therefore, a moral crisis as a country and as a people.

Thursday, July 11, 1963, in a radio and television address to the Nation.[139]

35rd
President of the
United States
(1961-1963)

John Fitzgerald
Kennedy
(1917-1963)

35rd
President of the
United States
(1961-1963)

John Fitzgerald
Kennedy
(1917-1963)

W̵e ask...that we may achieve in our time and for all time the ancient vision of peace on earth, goodwill toward men. That must always be our goal - and the righteousness of our cause must always underlie our strength. For as was written long ago, "Except the Lord keep the city, the watchman waketh but in vain."

Friday, November 22, 1963, the undelivered text of a speech he had planned to deliver at the Dallas Trade Mart, the day he was killed in an assassination plot.[140]

L et us here highly resolve that John Fitzgerald Kennedy did not live - or die - in vain. And on this Thanksgiving Eve, as we gather together to ask the Lord's blessings and give Him our thanks, let us unite in those familiar and cherished words:

> *America, America,*
> *God shed His grace on thee,*
> *And crown thy good*
> *With brotherhood*
> *From sea to shining sea.*

Wednesday, November 27, 1963, in his first address to Congress, upon assuming the Presidency.[141]

36th
President of the
United States
(1963-1969)

Lyndon Baines
Johnson
(1908-1973)

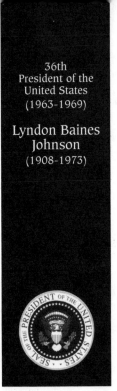

36th
President of the
United States
(1963-1969)

Lyndon Baines
Johnson
(1908-1973)

We have no promise from God that our greatness will endure. We have been allowed by Him to seek greatness with the sweat of our hands and the strength of our spirit....If we fail now, we shall have forgotten in abundance what we learned in hardship: that democracy rests on faith, that freedom asks more than it gives, and that the judgement of God is harshest on those who are most favored.

Wednesday, January 20, 1965, in his Inaugural
Address.[142]

Every family in America deserves a decent home....I have been criticized for such statements by people who think I raised hopes that can never be fulfilled, but I believe in the wisdom of the Bible - "Where there is no vision, the people perish."

Statement made in support of the Model Cities Act, passed by Congress in September of 1966.[143]

36th
President of the
United States
(1963-1969)

Lyndon Baines
Johnson
(1908-1973)

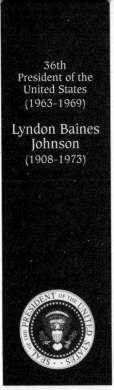

*I*n a moment of tragedy and trauma, the duties of this office fell upon me. I asked then for "your help and God's" that we might continue America on its course, binding up our wounds....America stands ready tonight to seek an honorable peace - and stands ready tonight to defend an honored cause - whatever the price, whatever the burden, whatever the sacrifice that duty may require. Thank you for listening. Good night and God bless all of you.

9:01 p.m., Sunday, March 31, 1968, in an address broadcast from the Oval Office.[144]

*O*nly a few short weeks ago we shared the glory of man's first sight of the world as God sees it, as a single sphere reflecting light in the darkness. As the Apollo astronauts flew over the moon's gray surface on Christmas Eve, they spoke to us of the beauty of earth - and in that voice so clear across the lunar distance, we heard them invoke God's blessing on its goodness.

Monday, January 20, 1969, in his First Inaugural Address.[145]

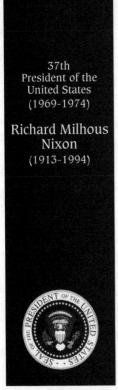

37th
President of the
United States
(1969-1974)

Richard Milhous
Nixon
(1913-1994)

)ask your prayers that in the years ahead I may have God's help in making decisions that are right for America, and I pray for your help so that together we may be worthy of our challenge....Let us go forward from here confident in hope, strong in our faith in one another, sustained by our faith in God who created us, and striving always to serve His purpose.

Saturday, January, 20, 1973, in his Second Inaugural Address.[146]

*A*s President, I must put the interest of America first. America needs a full-time President and a full-time Congress, particularly at this time with problems we face at home and abroad....To have served in this office is to have felt a very personal sense of kinship with each and every American. In leaving it, I do so with this prayer: May God's grace be with you in all the days ahead.

Thursday, August 8, 1974, in a televised address announcing his resignation.[147]

37th
President of the
United States
(1969-1974)

Richard Milhous
Nixon
(1913-1994)

37th
President of the
United States
(1969-1974)

Richard Milhous
Nixon
(1913-1994)

Mistakes, yes. But for personal gain, never. You did what you believed in. Sometimes right, sometimes wrong....Always remember others may hate you, but those who hate you don't win unless you hate them, and then you destroy yourself....I can only say to each and every one of you, we come from many faiths...but really the same God...you will be in our hearts and you will be in our prayers.

Thursday, August 8, 1974, in a private farewell to the members of his Cabinet, members of the White House Staff and friends.[148]

ask you to confirm me as your President with your prayers. And I hope that such prayers will also be the first of many....There is a Higher Power, by whatever name we honor Him, who ordains not only righteousness but love, not only justice but mercy. As we bind up the internal wounds...let us restore the Golden Rule to our political process.

Friday, August 9, 1974, in an address delivered upon assuming the Presidency after the resignation of President Nixon.[149]

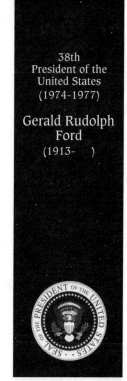

38th
President of the
United States
(1974-1977)

Gerald Rudolph
Ford
(1913-   )

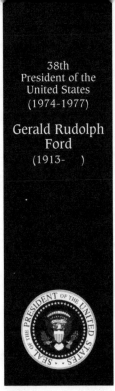

I am not here to make an Inaugural Address. The Nation needs action, not words. Nor will this be a formal report of the State of the Union. God willing, I will have at least three more chances to do that....I do not want a honeymoon with you. I want a good marriage.

Monday, August 12, 1974, in his First Address to Congress.[150]

𝒯 he Constitution is the supreme law of our land and it governs our actions as citizens. Only the laws of God, which govern our consciences, are superior to it. As we are a Nation under God, so I am sworn to uphold our laws with the help of God....I do believe, with all my heart and mind and spirit, that I, not as President, but as a humble servant of God, will receive justice without mercy if I fail to show mercy.

Sunday, September 8, 1974, in announcing his decision of pardon.[151]

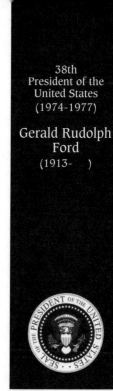

38th
President of the
United States
(1974-1977)

Gerald Rudolph
Ford
(1913-   )

153

Without God there could be no American form of government, nor an American way of life. Recognition of the Supreme Being is the first - the most basic - expression of Americanism. Thus the founding fathers of America saw it, and thus with God's help, it will continue to be.

Thursday, December 5, 1974, in a Proclamation of a National Day of Prayer.[152]

*H*ere before me is the Bible used in the inauguration of our first President in 1789, and I have just taken the oath of office on the Bible my mother gave me just a few years ago, opened to the timeless admonition from the ancient prophet Micah: "He hath showed thee, O man, what is good; and what does the Lord require of thee, but to do justly, and to love mercy, and to walk humbly with thy God."

Thursday, January 20, 1977, in his Inaugural Address.[153]

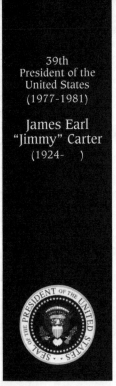

39th
President of the
United States
(1977-1981)

James Earl
"Jimmy" Carter
(1924-   )

O urs was the first society openly to define itself in terms of both spirituality and of human liberty. It is that unique self-definition which has given us an exceptional appeal, but it also imposes on us a special obligation, to take on those moral duties....I join in the hope that when my time as your President has ended, people might say this about our Nation: that we had remembered the words of Micah and renewed our search for humility, mercy, and justice.

Thursday, January 20, 1977, in his Inaugural Address.[154]

We feel that moral decay has weakened our country....It is now a time for healing. We want to have faith again!...Ours was the first nation to dedicate itself so clearly to basic moral and philosophical principles: That all people are created equal and endowed with inalienable rights to life, liberty, and the pursuit of happiness; and that the power of government is derived from the consent of the governed.

Thursday, July 15, 1976, in his Democratic acceptance speech, Madison Square Garden, New York City.[155]

39th
President of the
United States
(1977-1981)

James Earl
"Jimmy" Carter
(1924-   )

39th
President of the
United States
(1977-1981)

James Earl
"Jimmy" Carter
(1924-   )

We believe that the first time we're born, as children, it's human life given to us; and when we accept Jesus as our Savior, it's a new life. That's what "born again" means.

Tuesday, March 16, 1976, in an interview with Robert L. Turner during his Presidential campaign.[156]

I am told that tens of thousands of prayer meetings are being held on this day, and for that I am deeply grateful. We are a nation under God, and I believe God intended for us to be free....With God's help, we can and will resolve the problems which now confront us. And after all, why shouldn't we believe that? We are Americans. God bless you, and thank you.
Tuesday, January 20, 1981, in his First Inaugural Address.[157]

40th
President of the
United States
(1981-1989)

Ronald Wilson
Reagan
(1911-   )

40th
President of the
United States
(1981-1989)

Ronald Wilson
Reagan
(1911-   )

*N*OW, THEREFORE, be it Resolved by the Senate and House of Representatives of the United States of America in Congress assembled, That the President is authorized and requested to designate 1983 as a national "Year of the Bible" in recognition of both the formative influence the Bible has been for our Nation, and our national need to study and apply the teachings of the Holy Scriptures.

Monday, October 4, 1982, signed Joint Resolution of the 97th Congress, *Public Law 97-280.*[158]

*A*braham Lincoln said,.... "we have become...too proud to pray to the God that made us." Revived as an annual observance by Congress in 1952, the National Day of Prayer has become a great unifying force for our citizens.... This common expression of reverence heals and brings us together as a nation, and we pray it may one day bring renewed respect for God to all peoples of the world.

Thursday, January 27, 1983, in a Proclamation of a National Day of Prayer.[159]

40th
President of the
United States
(1981-1989)

Ronald Wilson
Reagan
(1911-   )

40th
President of the
United States
(1981-1989)

Ronald Wilson
Reagan
(1911-   )

*God bless you and welcome back....
I wonder if we could all join in a
moment of silent prayer....Amen....When
the first President, George Washington,
placed his hand upon the Bible, he stood
less than a single day's journey by
horseback from raw, untamed
wilderness....We stand together as we did
two centuries ago....One people under God
determined that our future shall be
worthy of our past.*

Monday, January 21, 1985, in his Second Inaugural
Address.[160]

I have just repeated word for word the oath taken by George Washington 200 years ago, and the Bible on which I place my hand is the Bible on which he place his....My first act as President is a prayer. I ask you to bow your heads: Heavenly Father, we bow our heads and thank You for Your love.... Make us strong to do Your work, willing to heed and hear Your will, and write on our hearts these words: "Use power to help people."...Help us to remember it, Lord. Amen.

Friday, January 20, 1989, in his Inaugural Address.[161]

41st
President of the
United States
(1989-1993)

George Herbert
Walker Bush
(1924-   )

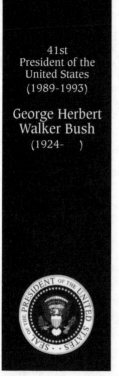

41st
President of the
United States
(1989-1993)

George Herbert
Walker Bush
(1924-   )

It was a biblical view of man - one affirming the dignity and worth of the human person, made in the Image of our Creator - that inspired the principles upon which the United States is founded....The Bible continues to give courage and direction to those who seek truth....I invite all Americans to discover the great inspiration and knowledge that can be obtained through thoughtful reading of the Bible.

Thursday, February 22, 1990, proclaimed 1990 the International Year of Bible Reading, as authorized by Congress, Senate Joint Resolution 164.[162]

*T*he great faith that led our Nation's Founding Fathers to pursue this bold experience in self-government has sustained us in uncertain and perilous times; it has given us strength and inspiration to this very day. Like them, we do very well to recall our "firm reliance on the protection of Divine Providence," to give thanks for the freedom and prosperity this Nation enjoys, and to pray for continued help and guidance from our wise and loving Creator.

Thursday, May 3, 1990, in a Proclamation of a National Day of Prayer.[163]

41st
President of the
United States
(1989-1993)

George Herbert
Walker Bush
(1924-   )

George Herbert
Walker Bush
(1924-   )

ℰach of us is invited to join in this National Day of Prayer. Indeed, although we may find our own words to express it, each of us can echo this timeless prayer of Solomon, the ancient king who prayed for, and received, the gift of wisdom: The Lord our God be with us, as He was with our fathers; may He not leave us or forsake us; so that He may incline our hearts to Him...that all the peoples of the earth may know that the Lord is God; there is no other.

In his 1992 National Day of Prayer Proclamation.[164]

*W*hen our Founders boldly declared America's Independence to the world and our purposes to the Almighty, they knew that America, to endure, would have to change....Let us begin with energy and hope, with faith and discipline, and let us work until our work is done. The Scripture says, "And let us not be weary in well-doing, for in due season, we shall reap, if we faint not."...With God's help, we must answer the call....

Wednesday, January 20, 1993, in his Inaugural Address.[165]

42st
President of the
United States
(1993-)

William Jefferson
"Bill" Clinton
(1946-)

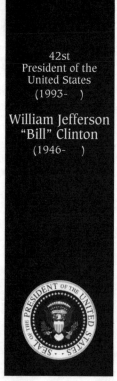

42st
President of the
United States
(1993-)

William Jefferson
"Bill" Clinton
(1946-)

If students can wear T-shirts advertising sports teams, rock groups or politicians, they can also wear T-shirts that promote religion....Religion is too important to our history and our heritage for us to keep it out of our schools....Nothing in the First Amendment converts our public schools into religion-free zones or requires all religious expression to be left behind at the schoolhouse door.

Wednesday, July 12, 1995, in an address at James Madison High School in Vienna, Virginia.[166]

Endnotes

[1] **George Washington.** April 30, 1789, Thursday, in his First Inaugural Address. National Archives, Original work and facsimile, (complete text), No. 22 (Washington: 1952). Jared Sparks, ed., *The Writings of George Washington* 12 vols. (Boston: American Stationer's Company, 1837, NY: F. Andrew's, 1834-1847), Vol. XII, pp. 2-5. James D. Richardson (U.S. Representative from Tennessee), ed., *A Compilation of the Messages and Papers of the Presidents 1789-1897*, 10 vols. (Washington, D.C.: U.S. Government Printing Office, published by Authority of Congress, 1897, 1899; Washington, D.C.: Bureau of National Literature and Art, *1789-1902*, 11 vols., 1907, 1910), Vol. 1, pp. 52-53. *Inaugural Addresses of the Presidents of the United States - From George Washington 1789 to Richard Milhous Nixon 1969* (Washington, D.C.: United States Government Printing Office; 91st Congress, 1st Session, House Document 91-142, 1969), pp. 1-4. Charles W. Eliot, LL.D., ed., *American Historical Documents 1000-1904* (New York: P.F. Collier & Son Company, *The Harvard Classics*, 1910), Vol. 43, pp. 241-245. William J. Johnson, *George Washington - The Christian* (St. Paul, MN: William J. Johnson, Merriam Park, February 23, 1919; Nashville, TN: Abingdon Press, 1919; reprinted Milford, MI: Mott Media, 1976; reprinted Arlington Heights, IL: Christian Liberty Press, 502 West Euclid Avenue, Arlington Heights, Illinois, 60004, 1992), pp. 161-162. John Clement Fitzpatrick, ed., *The Writings of George Washington, from the Original Manuscript Sources 1749-1799*, 39 vols. (Washington, D.C.: United States Government Printing Office, 1931-1944), Vol. XXX, pp. 291-296. William Barclay Allen, ed., *George Washington - A Collection* (Indianapolis: Liberty Classics, Liberty Fund, Inc., 7440 N. Shadeland, Indianapolis, Indiana 46250, 1988; based almost entirely on materials reproduced from *The Writings of George Washington from the original manuscript sources, 1745-1799* John Clement Fitzpatrick, editor), pp. 460-463. John F. Schroeder, ed., *Maxims of Washington* (Mt. Vernon: Mt. Vernon Ladies' Association, 1942), pp. 287-288. Saxe Commins, ed., *The Basic Writings of George Washington* (NY: Random House, 1948), complete work, pp. 599-602. Frederick C. Packard, Jr., ed., *Are You an American? - Great Americans Speak* (NY: Charles Scribner's Sons, 1951), pp. 14-18. Paul M. Angle, ed., *By These Words* (NY: Rand McNally & Company, 1954), pp. 128-131. Davis Newton Lott, *The Inaugural Addresses of the American Presidents* (NY: Holt, Rinehart and Winston, 1961), p. 3-5. Charles E. Rice, *The Supreme Court and Public Prayer* (New York: Fordham University Press, 1964), p. 177-178. Daniel Boorstin, Jr., ed., *An American Primer* (Chicago: The University of Chicago Press, 1966), complete work, pp. 172-174. Henry Steele Commager, ed., *Documents of American History*, 2 vols. (NY: F.S. Crofts and Company, 1934; Appleton-Century-Crofts, Inc., 1948, 6th edition, 1958; Englewood Cliffs, NJ: Prentice Hall, Inc., 9th edition, 1973), Vol. I, pp. 152-154. Gary DeMar, *God and Government, A Biblical and Historical Study* (Atlanta, GA: American Vision Press, 1984), p. 127-28. Pat Robertson, *America's Dates With Destiny* (Nashville, TN: Thomas Nelson Publishers, 1986), p. 104. Tim LaHaye, *Faith of Our Founding Fathers* (Brentwood, TN: Wolgemuth & Hyatt, Publishers, Inc., 1987), pp. 63-64, 107. John Eidsmoe, *Christianity and the Constitution - The Faith of Our Founding Fathers* (Grand Rapids, MI: Baker Book House, A Mott Media Book, 1987, 6th printing 1993), pp. 117, 123. David Barton, *The Myth of Separation* (Aledo, TX: WallBuilder Press, 1991), p. 113. "Our Christian Heritage," *Letter from Plymouth Rock* (Marlborough, NH: The Plymouth Rock Foundation), p. 4. D.P. Diffine, Ph.D., *One Nation Under God - How Close a Separation?* (Searcy, Arkansas: Harding University, Belden Center for Private Enterprise Education, 6th edition, 1992), p. 2. J. Michael Sharman, J.D., *Faith of the Fathers* (Culpeper, Virginia: Victory Publishing, 1995), pp. 18-19.

[2] **George Washington.** October 3, 1789, from the city of New York, President issued a Proclamation of a National Day of Thanksgiving. Jared Sparks, ed., *The Writings of George Washington* 12 vols. (Boston: American Stationer's Company, 1837, NY: F. Andrew's, 1834-1847), Vol. XII, p. 119. James D. Richardson (U.S. Representative from Tennessee), ed., *A Compilation of the Messages and Papers of the Presidents 1789-1897*, 10 vols. (Washington, D.C.: U.S. Government Printing Office, published by Authority of Congress, 1897, 1899; Washington, D.C.: Bureau of National Literature and Art, *1789-1902*, 11 vols., 1907, 1910), Vol. 1, p. 64. William J. Johnson, *George Washington - The Christian* (St. Paul, MN: William J. Johnson, Merriam Park, February 23, 1919; Nashville, TN: Abingdon Press, 1919; reprinted Milford, MI: Mott Media, 1976; reprinted Arlington Heights, IL: Christian Liberty Press, 502 West Euclid Avenue, Arlington Heights, Illinois, 60004, 1992), pp. 172-174. William Barclay Allen, ed., *George Washington - A Collection* (Indianapolis: Liberty Classics, Liberty Fund, Inc., 7440 N. Shadeland, Indianapolis, Indiana 46250, 1988; based almost entirely on materials reproduced from *The Writings of George Washington from the original manuscript sources, 1745-1799* John Clement Fitzpatrick, editor), pp. 534-353. John Clement Fitzpatrick, ed., *The Writings of George Washington, from the Original Manuscript Sources 1749-1799*, 39 vols. (Washington, D.C.: United States Government Printing Office, 1931-1944). John F. Schroeder, ed., *Maxims of Washington* (Mt. Vernon: Mt. Vernon Ladies' Association, 1942), pp. 275, 287. Anson

Phelps Stokes and Leo Pfeffer, *Church and State in the United States*, 3 vols. (NY: Harper & Brothers, 1950), p. 87. Pat Robertson, *America's Dates with Destiny* (Nashville: Thomas Nelson Publishers, 1986), p. 112. Tim LaHaye, *Faith of Our Founding Fathers* (Brentwood, TN: Wolgemuth & Hyatt, Publishers, Inc., 1987), pp. 104-106. John Eidsmoe, *Christianity and the Constitution - The Faith of Our Founding Fathers* (Grand Rapids, MI: Baker Book House, A Mott Media Book, 1987, 6th printing 1993), p. 118. David Barton, *The Myth of Separation* (Aledo, TX: WallBuilder Press, 1991), p. 115. Gary DeMar, *The Biblical Worldview* (Atlanta, GA: An American Vision Publication - American Vision, Inc., 1992), Vol. 8, No. 12, p. 8. D.P. Diffine, Ph.D., *One Nation Under God - How Close a Separation?* (Searcy, Arkansas: Harding University, Belden Center for Private Enterprise Education, 6th edition, 1992), p. 9. Gary DeMar, *America's Christian History: The Untold Story* (Atlanta, GA: American Vision Publishers, Inc., 1993), pp. 76-77.

[3] **George Washington.** January 1, 1795, from Philadelphia, in a Proclamation of a National Day of Public Thanksgiving and Prayer. Jared Sparks, ed., *The Writings of George Washington* 12 vols. (Boston: American Stationer's Company, 1837; NY: F. Andrew's, 1834-1847), Vol. XII, pp. 132-134. James D. Richardson (U.S. Representative from Tennessee), ed., *A Compilation of the Messages and Papers of the Presidents 1789-1897*, 10 vols. (Washington, D.C.: U.S. Government Printing Office, published by Authority of Congress, 1897, 1899; Washington, D.C.: Bureau of National Literature and Art, *1789-1902*, 11 vols., 1907, 1910), Vol. I, pp. 179-180. William J. Johnson, *George Washington - The Christian* (St. Paul, MN: William J. Johnson, Merriam Park, February 23, 1919; Nashville, TN: Abingdon Press, 1919; reprinted Milford, MI: Mott Media, 1976; reprinted Arlington Heights, IL: Christian Liberty Press, 502 West Euclid Avenue, Arlington Heights, Illinois, 60004, 1992), pp. 215-217. Catherine Millard, *The Rewriting of America's History* (Camp Hill, PA: Horizon House Publishers, 1991), pp. 61-62.

[4] **George Washington.** September 19, 1796, in his Farewell Address. *Address of George Washington, President of the United States, and Late Commander in Chief of the American Army, to the People of the United States, Preparatory to His Declination.* Published in the *American Daily Advertiser*, Philadelphia, September, 1796. Jared Sparks, ed., *The Writings of George Washington* 12 vols. (Boston: American Stationer's Company, 1837; NY: F. Andrew's, 1834-1847), Vol. XII, pp. 227-228. James D. Richardson (U.S. Representative from Tennessee), ed., *A Compilation of the Messages and Papers of the Presidents 1789-1897*, 10 vols. (Washington, D.C.: U.S. Government Printing Office, published by Authority of Congress, 1897, 1899; Washington, D.C.: Bureau of National Literature and Art, *1789-1902*, 11 vols., 1907, 1910), Vol. I, pp. 205-216, 220. William J. Johnson, *George Washington - The Christian* (St. Paul, MN: William J. Johnson, Merriam Park, February 23, 1919; Nashville, TN: Abingdon Press, 1919; reprinted Milford, MI: Mott Media, 1976; reprinted Arlington Heights, IL: Christian Liberty Press, 502 West Euclid Avenue, Arlington Heights, Illinois, 60004, 1992), pp. 217-219. John Clement Fitzpatrick, ed., *The Writings of George Washington, from the Original Manuscript Sources 1749-1799*, 39 vols. (Washington, D.C.: United States Government Printing Office, 1931-1944), Vol. 35, p. 229. Henry Steele Commager, ed., *Documents of American History*, 2 vols. (NY: F.S. Crofts and Company, 1934; Appleton-Century-Crofts, Inc., 1948, 6th edition, 1958; Englewood Cliffs, NJ: Prentice Hall, Inc., 9th edition, 1973), Vol. I, pp. 169-173. William Barclay Allen, ed., *George Washington - A Collection* (Indianapolis: Liberty Classics, Liberty Fund, Inc., 7440 N. Shadeland, Indianapolis, Indiana 46250, 1988; based almost entirely on materials reproduced from *The Writings of George Washington from the original manuscript sources, 1745-1799/*John Clement Fitzpatrick, ed.), pp. 512-527. Charles W. Eliot, LL.D., ed., *American Historical Documents 1000-1904* (New York: P.F. Collier & Son Company, *The Harvard Classics*, 1910), Vol. 43, pp. 250-266. John F. Schroeder, ed., *Maxims of Washington* (Mt. Vernon: Mt. Vernon Ladies' Association, 1942), pp. 286-287. Saxe Commins, ed., *The Basic Writings of George Washington* (NY: Random House, 1948), complete work, pp. 636-643. Frederick C. Packard, Jr., ed., *Are You an American? - Great Americans Speak* (NY: Charles Scribner's Sons, 1951), p. 2. Paul M. Angle, ed., *By These Words* (NY: Rand McNally & Company, 1954), pp. 138, 145, 146. Richard D. Heffner, *A Documentary History of the United States* (New York: The New American Library of World Literature, Inc., 1961), pp. 60-67. Daniel Boorstin, Jr., ed., *An American Primer* (Chicago: The University of Chicago Press, 1966), complete work, pp. 197-207. Lillian W. Kay, ed., *The Ground on Which We Stand - Basic Documents of American History* (NY: Franklin Watts., 1969), pp. 123-125. John Eidsmoe, *God and Caesar* (Westchester, IL: Crossway Books, 1984), p. 22. John Eidsmoe, *Christianity and the Constitution - The Faith of Our Founding Fathers* (Grand Rapids, MI: Baker Book House, A Mott Media Book, 1987, 6th printing 1993), p. 119. Tim LaHaye, *Faith of Our Founding Fathers* (Brentwood, TN: Wolgemuth & Hyatt, Inc., 1987), pp. 91, 105-106. Ronald Reid, ed., *Three Centuries of American Rhetorical Discourse - An Anthology and a Review* (Prospect Heights, IL: Waveland Press, Inc., 1988), pp. 187-201. David Barton, *The Myth of Separation* (Aledo, TX: WallBuilder Press, 1991), pp. 115-116, 124. William Safire, ed., *Lend Me Your Ears - Great Speeches in History* (NY: W.W. Norton & Company 1992), p. 359-365. D.P. Diffine, Ph.D.,

170

One Nation Under God - How Close a Separation? (Searcy, Arkansas: Harding University, 6th edition, Belden Center for Private Enterprise Education, 1992), p. 9. Rush H. Limbaugh III, See, I Told You So (New York, NY: reprinted by permission of Pocket Books, a division of Simon & Schuster Inc., 1993), pp. 73-76. Stephen McDowell and Mark Beliles, "The Providential Perspective" (Charlottesville, VA: The Providence Foundation, P.O. Box 6759, Charlottesville, Va. 22906, January 1994), Vol. 9, No. 1, p. 4.

[5] **John Adams.** March 4, 1797, Saturday, in his Inaugural Address, given in Philadelphia, Pennsylvania. James D. Richardson (U.S. Representative from Tennessee), ed., A Compilation of the Messages and Papers of the Presidents 1789-1897, 10 vols. (Washington, D.C.: U.S. Government Printing Office, published by Authority of Congress, 1897, 1899; Washington, D.C.: Bureau of National Literature and Art, 1789-1902, 11 vols., 1907, 1910), Vol. I, pp. 228-232. Inaugural Addresses of the Presidents of the United States - From George Washington 1789 to Richard Milhous Nixon 1969 (Washington, D.C.: United States Government Printing Office; 91st Congress, 1st Session, House Document 91-142, 1969), pp. 7-11. Charles E. Rice, The Supreme Court and Public Prayer (New York: Fordham University Press, 1964), pp. 178-179. Proclaim Liberty (Dallas, TX: Word of Faith), p. 1. J. Michael Sharman, J.D., Faith of the Fathers (Culpepper, Virginia: Victory Publishing, 1995), p. 22.

[6] **John Adams.** March 23, 1798, in a Proclamation of a National Day of Humiliation, Fasting, and Prayer. James D. Richardson (U.S. Representative from Tennessee), ed., A Compilation of the Messages and Papers of the Presidents 1789-1897, 10 vols. (Washington, D.C.: U.S. Government Printing Office, published by Authority of Congress, 1897, 1899; Washington, D.C.: Bureau of National Literature and Art, 1789-1902, 11 vols., 1907, 1910). Vol. I, pp. 268-270. Benjamin Franklin Morris, The Christian Life and Character of the Civil Institutions of the United States (Philadelphia: George W. Childs, 1864), pp. 545-546. Stephen McDowell and Mark Beliles, "The Providential Perspective" (Charlottesville, VA: The Providence Foundation, P.O. Box 6759, Charlottesville, Va. 22906, January 1994), Vol. 9, No. 1, p. 6.

[7] **John Adams.** March 6, 1799, in a Proclamation of a National Day of Humiliation, Fasting, and Prayer. James D. Richardson (U.S. Representative from Tennessee), ed., A Compilation of the Messages and Papers of the Presidents 1789-1897, 10 vols. (Washington, D.C.: U.S. Government Printing Office, published by Authority of Congress, 1897, 1899; Washington, D.C.: Bureau of National Literature and Art, 1789-1902, 11 vols., 1907, 1910), Vol. 1, pp. 284-286. Benjamin Franklin Morris, The Christian Life and Character of the Civil Institutions of the United States (Philadelphia: George W. Childs, 1864), pp. 547-548. Gary DeMar, The Biblical Worldview (Atlanta, GA: An American Vision Publication - American Vision, Inc., 1992), Vol. 8, No. 12, p. 9. Gary DeMar, America's Christian History: The Untold Story (Atlanta, GA: American Vision Publishers, Inc., 1993), p. 78. Stephen McDowell and Mark Beliles, "The Providential Perspective" (Charlottesville, VA: The Providence Foundation, P.O. Box 6759, Charlottesville, Va. 22906, January 1994), Vol. 9, No. 1, pp. 4, 6.

[8] **John Adams.** November 22, 1800, in his Fourth Annual Address to Congress, which began the first session of Congress in the new Capitol of Washington, D.C. James D. Richardson (U.S. Representative from Tennessee), ed., A Compilation of the Messages and Papers of the Presidents 1789-1897, 10 vols. (Washington, D.C.: U.S. Government Printing Office, published by Authority of Congress, 1897, 1899; Washington, D.C.: Bureau of National Literature and Art, 1789-1902, 11 vols., 1907, 1910), Vol. I, p. 305.

[9] **Thomas Jefferson.** March 4, 1801, Wednesday, in his First Inaugural Address. James D. Richardson (U.S. Representative from Tennessee), ed., A Compilation of the Messages and Papers of the Presidents 1789-1897, 10 vols. (Washington, D.C.: U.S. Government Printing Office, published by Authority of Congress, 1897, 1899; Washington, D.C.: Bureau of National Literature and Art, 1789-1902, 11 vols., 1907, 1910), Vol. I, p. 322-324. Inaugural Addresses of the Presidents of the United States - From George Washington 1789 to Richard Milhous Nixon 1969 (Washington, D.C.: United States Government Printing Office; 91st Congress, 1st Session, House Document 91-142, 1969), pp. 13-16. H.A. Washington, ed., The Writings of Thomas Jefferson - Being His Autobiography, Correspondence, Reports, Messages, Addresses, and Other Writings, Official and Private, 9 vols. (NY: Derby & Jackson, 1859; Washington, 1853-54; Philadelphia, 1871), Vol. VIII, p. 6. Henry Steele Commager, ed., Documents of American History, 2 vols. (NY: F.S. Crofts and Company, 1934; Appleton-Century-Crofts, Inc., 1948, 6th edition, 1958; Englewood Cliffs, NJ: Prentice Hall, Inc., 9th edition, 1973), Vol. I, pp. 187-189. Frederick C. Packard, Jr., ed., Are You an American? - Great Americans Speak (NY: Charles Scribner's Sons, 1951), p. 21-24. Paul M. Angle, ed., By These Words (NY: Rand McNally & Company, 1954), pp. 157-159. Charles Hurd, ed.,

A Treasury of Great American Speeches (NY: Hawthorne Books, 1959), p. 50. Richard D. Heffner, *A Documentary History of the United States* (New York: The New American Library of World Literature, Inc., 1961), pp. 71-74. Davis Newton Lott, *The Inaugural Addresses of the American Presidents* (NY: Holt, Rinehart and Winston, 1961), p. 16-17. Charles E. Rice, *The Supreme Court and Public Prayer* (New York: Fordham University Press, 1964), p. 179. William Safire, ed., *Lend Me Your Ears - Great Speeches in History* (NY: W.W. Norton & Company 1992), pp. 727-729. J. Michael Sharman, J.D., *Faith of the Fathers* (Culpepper, Virginia: Victory Publishing, 1995), p. 24.

[10] **Thomas Jefferson.** December 8, 1801, in his First Annual Message to Congress. James D. Richardson (U.S. Representative from Tennessee), ed., *A Compilation of the Messages and Papers of the Presidents 1789-1897*, 10 vols. (Washington, D.C.: U.S. Government Printing Office, published by Authority of Congress, 1897, 1899; Washington, D.C.: Bureau of National Literature and Art, *1789-1902*, 11 vols., 1907, 1910), Vol. I, p. 326. Richard Maxfield, K. De Lynn Cook, and W. Cleon Skousen, *The Real Thomas Jefferson* (Washington, D.C.: National Center for Constitutional Studies, 2nd edition, 1981, 1983), p. 404. John Eidsmoe, *Christianity and The Constitution - The Faith of Our Founding Fathers* (Grand Rapids, MI: Baker Book House, 1987), p. 228.

[11] **Thomas Jefferson.** December 15, 1802, in his Second Annual Message to Congress. James D. Richardson (U.S. Representative from Tennessee), ed., *A Compilation of the Messages and Papers of the Presidents 1789-1897*, 10 vols. (Washington, D.C.: U.S. Government Printing Office, published by Authority of Congress, 1897, 1899; Washington, D.C.: Bureau of National Literature and Art, *1789-1902*, 11 vols., 1907, 1910), Vol. I, pp. 342-345.

[12] **Thomas Jefferson.** March 4, 1805, Monday, in his Second Inaugural Address. James D. Richardson (U.S. Representative from Tennessee), ed., *A Compilation of the Messages and Papers of the Presidents 1789-1897*, 10 vols. (Washington, D.C.: U.S. Government Printing Office, published by Authority of Congress, 1897, 1899; Washington, D.C.: Bureau of National Literature and Art, *1789-1902*, 11 vols., 1907, 1910), Vol. I, pp. 378-382. *Inaugural Addresses of the Presidents of the United States - From George Washington 1789 to Richard Milhous Nixon 1969* (Washington, D.C.: United States Government Printing Office; 91st Congress, 1st Session, House Document 91-142, 1969), pp. 17-21. Saul K. Padover, ed., *The Complete Jefferson, Containing His Major Writings, Published and Unpublished, Except His Letters* (NY: Duell, Sloan & Pearce, 1943), p. 412. Adrienne Koch and William Paden, eds., *The Life and Selected Writings of Thomas Jefferson* (NY: Random House, 1944), p. 341. Davis Newton Lott, *The Inaugural Addresses of the American Presidents* (NY: Holt, Rinehart and Winston, 1961), p. 22. Charles E. Rice, *The Supreme Court and Public Prayer* (New York: Fordham University Press, 1964), p. 179. Arthur Schlesinger Jr., ed., *The Chief Executive* (NY: Chelsea House Publishers, 1965), p. 20. Richard Maxfield, K. De Lynn Cook, and W. Cleon Skousen, *The Real Thomas Jefferson* (Washington, D.C.: National Center for Constitutional Studies, 2nd edition, 1981, 1983), pp. 403-440. Gary DeMar, *God and Government - A Biblical and Historical Study* (Atlanta, GA: American Vision Press, 1982), p. 166. John Eidsmoe, *Christianity and The Constitution - The Faith of Our Founding Fathers* (Grand Rapids, MI: Baker Book House, 1987), pp. 227-228, 243. David Barton, *The Myth of Separation* (Aledo, TX: WallBuilder Press, 1991), pp. 42, 174. John Whitehead, *The Rights of Religious Persons in Public Education* (Wheaton, IL: Crossway Books, Good News Publishers, 1991), p. 45. Catherine Millard, *The Rewriting of America's History* (Camp Hill, PA: Horizon House Publishers, 1991), pp. 91-92. Gary DeMar, *America's Christian History: The Untold Story* (Atlanta, GA: American Vision Publishers, Inc., 1993), p. 116. J. Michael Sharman, J.D., *Faith of the Fathers* (Culpepper, Virginia: Victory Publishing, 1995), pp. 25-26.

[13] **James Madison.** March 4, 1809, Saturday, in his First Inaugural Address. James D. Richardson (U.S. Representative from Tennessee), ed., *A Compilation of the Messages and Papers of the Presidents 1789-1897*, 10 vols. (Washington, D.C.: U.S. Government Printing Office, published by Authority of Congress, 1897, 1899; Washington, D.C.: Bureau of National Literature and Art, *1789-1902*, 11 vols., 1907, 1910), Vol. I, pp. 466-468. Irving Brant, *James Madison* (Indianapolis: Bobbs-Merrill, 1941), Vol. V, p. 19. *Inaugural Addresses of the Presidents of the United States - From George Washington 1789 to Richard Milhous Nixon 1969* (Washington, D.C.: United States Government Printing Office; 91st Congress, 1st Session, House Document 91-142, 1969), pp. 23-25. Davis Newton Lott, *The Inaugural Addresses of the American Presidents* (NY: Holt, Rinehart and Winston, 1961), p. 27. Charles E. Rice, *The Supreme Court and Public Prayer* (New York: Fordham University Press, 1964), pp. 179-180. Arthur M. Schlesinger, *The State of the Union Messages of the Presidents, 1790-1966* (New York: Chelsea House-Robert Hector, 1966); Adrienne Koch, *Madison's "Advice to My Country"* (Princeton: Princeton University Press, 1966), p. 43. Tim LaHaye, *Faith of Our Founding Fathers* (Brentwood, TN: Wolgemuth & Hyatt, Publishers, Inc., 1987), p. 131. *Proclaim Liberty* (Dallas, TX: Word of Faith), p. 1. John Eidsmoe, *Christianity and the Constitution - The Faith of Our Founding*

Fathers (Grand Rapids, MI: Baker Book House, A Mott Media Book, 1987, 6th printing 1993), p. 110. J. Michael Sharman, J.D., *Faith of the Fathers* (Culpepper, Virginia: Victory Publishing, 1995), p. 28.

[14] **James Madison.** July 9, 1812, in a Proclamation of a National Day of Public Humiliation and Prayer. James D. Richardson (U.S. Representative from Tennessee), ed., *A Compilation of the Messages and Papers of the Presidents 1789-1897*, 10 vols. (Washington, D.C.: U.S. Government Printing Office, published by Authority of Congress, 1897, 1899; Washington, D.C.: Bureau of National Literature and Art, *1789-1902*, 11 vols., 1907, 1910), Vol. I, p. 513. Benjamin Franklin Morris, *The Christian Life and Character of the Civil Institutions of the United States* (Philadelphia: George W. Childs, 1864), p. 549. Irving Brant, *James Madison* (Indianapolis: Bobbs-Merrill, 1941), Vol. V, p. 19; Vol. VI, p. 28. John Eidsmoe, *Christianity and The Constitution - The Faith of Our Founding Fathers* (Baker Book House, 1987), p. 111. -

[15] **James Madison.** March 4, 1813, Thursday, in his Second Inaugural Address. James D. Richardson (U.S. Representative from Tennessee), ed., *A Compilation of the Messages and Papers of the Presidents 1789-1897*, 10 vols. (Washington, D.C.: U.S. Government Printing Office, published by Authority of Congress, 1897, 1899; Washington, D.C.: Bureau of National Literature and Art, *1789-1902*, 11 vols., 1907, 1910), Vol. I, p. 524. *Inaugural Addresses of the Presidents of the United States - From George Washington 1789 to Richard Milhous Nixon 1969* (Washington, D.C.: United States Government Printing Office; 91st Congress, 1st Session, House Document 91-142, 1969), pp. 26-28. Charles E. Rice, *The Supreme Court and Public Prayer* (New York: Fordham University Press, 1964), p. 180. J. Michael Sharman, J.D., *Faith of the Fathers* (Culpepper, Virginia: Victory Publishing, 1995), p. 29.

[16] **James Madison.** July 23, 1813, in a Proclamation of a National Day of Public Humiliation and Prayer. James D. Richardson (U.S. Representative from Tennessee), ed., *A Compilation of the Messages and Papers of the Presidents 1789-1897*, 10 vols. (Washington, D.C.: U.S. Government Printing Office, published by Authority of Congress, 1897, 1899; Washington, D.C.: Bureau of National Literature and Art, *1789-1902*, 11 vols., 1907, 1910), Vol. I, pp. 532-533. Irving Brant, *James Madison* (Indianapolis: Bobbs-Merrill, 1941), V:19, VI:198. John Eidsmoe, *Christianity and the Constitution - The Faith of Our Founding Fathers* (Grand Rapids, MI: Baker Book House, A Mott Media Book, 1987, 6th printing 1993), p. 111.

[17] **James Monroe.** March 4, 1817, Tuesday, in his First Inaugural Address, delivered on the steps of the Capitol. James D. Richardson (U.S. Representative from Tennessee), ed., *A Compilation of the Messages and Papers of the Presidents 1789-1897*, 10 vols. (Washington, D.C.: U.S. Government Printing Office, published by Authority of Congress, 1897, 1899; Washington, D.C.: Bureau of National Literature and Art, *1789-1902*, 11 vols., 1907, 1910), Vol. II, pp. 4-10. *Inaugural Addresses of the Presidents of the United States - From George Washington 1789 to Richard Milhous Nixon 1969* (Washington, D.C.: United States Government Printing Office; 91st Congress, 1st Session, House Document 91-142, 1969), pp. 29-36. Davis Newton Lott, *The Inaugural Addresses of the American Presidents* (NY: Holt, Rinehart and Winston, 1961), p. 38. Charles E. Rice, *The Supreme Court and Public Prayer* (New York: Fordham University Press, 1964), p. 180. Arthur Schlesinger Jr., ed., *The Chief Executive* (NY: Chelsea House Publishers, 1965), pp. 33-34. J. Michael Sharman, J.D., *Faith of the Fathers* (Culpepper, Virginia: Victory Publishing, 1995), pp. 31-32.

[18] **James Monroe.** November 14, 1820, in his Fourth Annual Message to Congress. James D. Richardson (U.S. Representative from Tennessee), ed., *A Compilation of the Messages and Papers of the Presidents 1789-1897*, 10 vols. (Washington, D.C.: U.S. Government Printing Office, published by Authority of Congress, 1897, 1899; Washington, D.C.: Bureau of National Literature and Art, *1789-1902*, 11 vols., 1907, 1910), Vol. II, pp. 74-75.

[19] **James Monroe.** March 5, 1821, Monday, in his Second Inaugural Address. James D. Richardson (U.S. Representative from Tennessee), ed., *A Compilation of the Messages and Papers of the Presidents 1789-1897*, 10 vols. (Washington, D.C.: U.S. Government Printing Office, published by Authority of Congress, 1897, 1899; Washington, D.C.: Bureau of National Literature and Art, *1789-1902*, 11 vols., 1907, 1910), Vol. II, pp. 86-94. *Inaugural Addresses of the Presidents of the United States - From George Washington 1789 to Richard Milhous Nixon 1969* (Washington, D.C.: United States Government Printing Office; 91st Congress, 1st Session, House Document 91-142, 1969), pp. 37-45. Davis Newton Lott, *The Inaugural Addresses of the American Presidents* (NY: Holt, Rinehart and Winston, 1961), p. 48. Charles E. Rice, *The Supreme Court and Public Prayer* (New York: Fordham University Press, 1964), pp. 180-181. J. Michael Sharman, J.D., *Faith of the Fathers* (Culpepper, Virginia: Victory Publishing, 1995), p. 33.

[20] **James Monroe.** December 7, 1824, in his Eighth Annual Message to Congress. James D. Richardson (U.S. Representative from Tennessee), ed., *A Compilation of the Messages and Papers of the Presidents 1789-1897*, 10 vols. (Washington, D.C.: U.S. Government Printing Office, published by Authority of Congress, 1897, 1899; Washington, D.C.: Bureau of National Literature and Art, *1789-1902*, 11 vols., 1907, 1910), Vol. II, pp. 248, 263-264.

[21] **John Quincy Adams.** March 4, 1825, Friday, in his First Inaugural Address, delivered on the steps of the Capitol. James D. Richardson (U.S. Representative from Tennessee), ed., *A Compilation of the Messages and Papers of the Presidents 1789-1897*, 10 vols. (Washington, D.C.: U.S. Government Printing Office, published by Authority of Congress, 1897, 1899; Washington, D.C.: Bureau of National Literature and Art, *1789-1902*, 11 vols., 1907, 1910), Vol. II, pp. 294-299. *Inaugural Addresses of the Presidents of the United States - From George Washington 1789 to Richard Milhous Nixon 1969* (Washington, D.C.: United States Government Printing Office; 91st Congress, 1st Session, House Document 91-142, 1969), pp. 47-53. Davis Newton Lott, *The Inaugural Addresses of the American Presidents* (NY: Holt, Rinehart and Winston, 1961), p. 51. Charles E. Rice, *The Supreme Court and Public Prayer* (New York: Fordham University Press, 1964), p. 181. Arthur Schlesinger Jr., ed., *The Chief Executive* (NY: Chelsea House Publishers, 1965), p. 53. Benjamin Weiss, *God in American History: A Documentation of America's Religious Heritage* (Grand Rapids, MI: Zondervan, 1966), p. 68. *The Annals of America*, 20 vols. (Chicago, IL: Encyclopedia Britannica, 1968), Vol. 5, p. 138. Willard Cantelon, *Money Master of the World* (Plainfield, NJ: Logos International, 1976), p. 120. J. Michael Sharman, J.D., *Faith of the Fathers* (Culpepper, Virginia: Victory Publishing, 1995), pp. 35-36.

[22] **John Quincy Adams.** December 6, 1825, in his First Annual Message to Congress. James D. Richardson (U.S. Representative from Tennessee), ed., *A Compilation of the Messages and Papers of the Presidents 1789-1897*, 10 vols. (Washington, D.C.: U.S. Government Printing Office, published by Authority of Congress, 1897, 1899; Washington, D.C.: Bureau of National Literature and Art, *1789-1902*, 11 vols., 1907, 1910), Vol. II, pp. 299-300, 311-312, 316-317. Henry Steele Commager, ed., *Documents of American History*, 2 vols. (NY: F.S. Crofts and Company, 1934; Appleton-Century-Crofts, Inc., 1948, 6th edition, 1958; Englewood Cliffs, NJ: Prentice Hall, Inc., 9th edition, 1973), Vol. I, p. 242.

[23] **John Quincy Adams.** December 5, 1826, in his Second Annual Message to Congress. James D. Richardson (U.S. Representative from Tennessee), ed., *A Compilation of the Messages and Papers of the Presidents 1789-1897*, 10 vols. (Washington, D.C.: U.S. Government Printing Office, published by Authority of Congress, 1897, 1899; Washington, D.C.: Bureau of National Literature and Art, *1789-1902*, 11 vols., 1907, 1910), Vol. II, pp. 350, 364.

[24] **John Quincy Adams.** December 2, 1828, in his Fourth Annual Message to Congress. James D. Richardson (U.S. Representative from Tennessee), ed., *A Compilation of the Messages and Papers of the Presidents 1789-1897*, 10 vols. (Washington, D.C.: U.S. Government Printing Office, published by Authority of Congress, 1897, 1899; Washington, D.C.: Bureau of National Literature and Art, *1789-1902*, 11 vols., 1907, 1910), Vol. II, pp. 407, 412, 415-416.

[25] **Andrew Jackson.** March 4, 1829, Wednesday, in his First Inaugural Address. James D. Richardson (U.S. Representative from Tennessee), ed., *A Compilation of the Messages and Papers of the Presidents 1789-1897*, 10 vols. (Washington, D.C.: U.S. Government Printing Office, published by Authority of Congress, 1897, 1899; Washington, D.C.: Bureau of National Literature and Art, *1789-1902*, 11 vols., 1907, 1910), Vol. II, p. 438. *Inaugural Addresses of the Presidents of the United States - From George Washington 1789 to Richard Milhous Nixon 1969* (Washington, D.C.: United States Government Printing Office; 91st Congress, 1st Session, House Document 91-142, 1969), pp. 55-57. Davis Newton Lott, *The Inaugural Addresses of the American Presidents* (NY: Holt, Rinehart and Winston, 1961), p. 59. Charles E. Rice, *The Supreme Court and Public Prayer* (New York: Fordham University Press, 1964), p. 181. Arthur Schlesinger Jr., ed., *The Chief Executive* (NY: Chelsea House Publishers, 1965), p. 62. J. Michael Sharman, J.D., *Faith of the Fathers* (Culpepper, Virginia: Victory Publishing, 1995), p. 38.

[26] **Andrew Jackson.** January 20, 1830, in a message to Congress. James D. Richardson (U.S. Representative from Tennessee), ed., *A Compilation of the Messages and Papers of the Presidents 1789-1897*, 10 vols. (Washington, D.C.: U.S. Government Printing Office, published by Authority of Congress, 1897, 1899; Washington, D.C.: Bureau of National Literature and Art, *1789-1902*, 11 vols., 1907, 1910), Vol. II, p. 468.

[27] **Andrew Jackson.** March 4, 1833, in his Inaugural Address. James D. Richardson (U.S. Representative from Tennessee), ed., *A Compilation of the Messages and Papers of the Presidents 1789-1897*, 10 vols. (Washington, D.C.: U.S. Government Printing Office, published by Authority of Congress, 1897, 1899; Washington, D.C.: Bureau of National Literature and Art, *1789-1902*, 11 vols., 1907, 1910), Vol. III, p. 5. *Inaugural Addresses of the Presidents of the United States - From George Washington 1789 to Richard Milhous Nixon 1969* (Washington, D.C.: United States Government Printing Office; 91st Congress, 1st Session, House Document 91-142,

1969), pp. 58-60. Davis Newton Lott, *The Inaugural Addresses of the American Presidents* (NY: Holt, Rinehart and Winston, 1961), p. 63. Charles E. Rice, *The Supreme Court and Public Prayer* (New York: Fordham University Press, 1964), p. 181. Arthur Schlesinger Jr., ed., *The Chief Executive* (NY: Chelsea House Publishers, 1965) p. 67. Benjamin Weiss, *God in American History: A Documentation of America's Religious Heritage* (Grand Rapids, MI: Zondervan, 1966), p. 73. Willard Cantelon, *Money Master of the World* (Plainfield, NJ: Logos International, 1976), p. 120. *Proclaim Liberty* (Dallas, TX: Word of Faith), p. 1. J. Michael Sharman, J.D., *Faith of the Fathers* (Culpepper, Virginia: Victory Publishing, 1995), p. 39.

[98] **Andrew Jackson.** April 15, 1834, in a Protest message to the Senate. James D. Richardson (U.S. Representative from Tennessee), ed., *A Compilation of the Messages and Papers of the Presidents 1789-1897*, 10 vols. (Washington, D.C.: U.S. Government Printing Office, published by Authority of Congress, 1897, 1899; Washington, D.C.: Bureau of National Literature and Art, *1789-1902*, 11 vols., 1907, 1910), Vol. II, pp. 87, 92-93.

[99] **Martin Van Buren.** March 4, 1837, Saturday, in his Inaugural Address. James D. Richardson (U.S. Representative from Tennessee), ed., *A Compilation of the Messages and Papers of the Presidents 1789-1897*, 10 vols. (Washington, D.C.: U.S. Government Printing Office, published by Authority of Congress, 1897, 1899; Washington, D.C.: Bureau of National Literature and Art, *1789-1902*, 11 vols., 1907, 1910), Vol. III, pp. 313-320. Benjamin Franklin Morris, *The Christian Life and Character of the Civil Institutions of the United States* (Philadelphia: George W. Childs, 1864), p. 604. *Inaugural Addresses of the Presidents of the United States - From George Washington 1789 to Richard Milhous Nixon 1969* (Washington, D.C.: United States Government Printing Office; 91st Congress, 1st Session, House Document 91-142, 1969), pp. 61-69. Charles E. Rice, *The Supreme Court and Public Prayer* (New York: Fordham University Press, 1964), p. 182. Stephen Abbott Northrop, D.D., *A Cloud of Witnesses* (Portland, OR: American Heritage Ministries, 1987; Mantle Ministries, 228 Still Ridge, Bulverde, Texas), p. 473. J. Michael Sharman, J.D., *Faith of the Fathers* (Culpepper, Virginia: Victory Publishing, 1995), p. 41.

[30] **Martin Van Buren.** September 4, 1837, in a Special Session Message to Congress. James D. Richardson (U.S. Representative from Tennessee), ed., *A Compilation of the Messages and Papers of the Presidents 1789-1897*, 10 vols. (Washington, D.C.: U.S. Government Printing Office, published by Authority of Congress, 1897, 1899; Washington, D.C.: Bureau of National Literature and Art, *1789-1902*, 11 vols., 1907, 1910), Vol. III, pp. 331-346.

[31] **Martin Van Buren.** December 2, 1839, in his Third Annual Message to Congress. James D. Richardson (U.S. Representative from Tennessee), ed., *A Compilation of the Messages and Papers of the Presidents 1789-1897*, 10 vols. (Washington, D.C.: U.S. Government Printing Office, published by Authority of Congress, 1897, 1899; Washington, D.C.: Bureau of National Literature and Art, *1789-1902*, 11 vols., 1907, 1910), Vol. III, pp. 529-530, 553-554.

[32] **Martin Van Buren.** December 5, 1840, in his Fourth Annual Message to Congress. James D. Richardson (U.S. Representative from Tennessee), ed., *A Compilation of the Messages and Papers of the Presidents 1789-1897*, 10 vols. (Washington, D.C.: U.S. Government Printing Office, published by Authority of Congress, 1897, 1899; Washington, D.C.: Bureau of National Literature and Art, *1789-1902*, 11 vols., 1907, 1910), Vol. III, p. 602.

[33] **William Henry Harrison.** March 4, 1841, Thursday, in his Inaugural Address. James D. Richardson (U.S. Representative from Tennessee), ed., *A Compilation of the Messages and Papers of the Presidents 1789-1897*, 10 vols. (Washington, D.C.: U.S. Government Printing Office, published by Authority of Congress, 1897, 1899; Washington, D.C.: Bureau of National Literature and Art, *1789-1902*, 11 vols., 1907, 1910), Vol. 4, pp. 6-20. Benjamin Franklin Morris, *The Christian Life and Character of the Civil Institutions of the United States* (Philadelphia: George W. Childs, 1864), p. 605. *Inaugural Addresses of the Presidents of the United States - From George Washington 1789 to Richard Milhous Nixon 1969* (Washington, D.C.: United States Government Printing Office; 91st Congress, 1st Session, House Document 91-142, 1969), pp. 71-87. Davis Newton Lott, *The Inaugural Addresses of the American Presidents* (NY: Holt, Rinehart and Winston, 1961), p. 86. Charles E. Rice, *The Supreme Court and Public Prayer* (New York: Fordham University Press, 1964), p. 182. Arthur Schlesinger Jr., ed., *The Chief Executive* (NY: Chelsea House Publishers, 1965), pp. 93-94. Stephen Abbott Northrop, D.D., *A Cloud of Witnesses* (Portland, Oregon: American Heritage Ministries, 1987; Mantle Ministries, 228 Still Ridge, Bulverde, Texas), p. 215. Peter Marshall and David Manuel, *The Glory of America* (Bloomington, MN: Garborg's Heart 'N Home, Inc., 1991), 4.4. J. Michael Sharman, J.D., *Faith of the Fathers* (Culpepper, Virginia: Victory Publishing, 1995), pp. 43-44.

[34] **William Henry Harrison.** March 4, 1841, Thursday, in his Inaugural Address. James D. Richardson (U.S. Representative from Tennessee), ed., *A Compilation of the Messages and Papers of the Presidents 1789-1897*, 10 vols. (Washington, D.C.: U.S. Government Printing Office, published by Authority of Congress, 1897, 1899;

Washington, D.C.: Bureau of National Literature and Art, *1789-1902*, 11 vols., 1907, 1910), Vol. 4, pp. 6-20. Benjamin Franklin Morris, *The Christian Life and Character of the Civil Institutions of the United States* (Philadelphia: George W. Childs, 1864), p. 605. *Inaugural Addresses of the Presidents of the United States - From George Washington 1789 to Richard Milhous Nixon 1969* (Washington, D.C.: United States Government Printing Office; 91st Congress, 1st Session, House Document 91-142, 1969), pp. 71-87. Davis Newton Lott, *The Inaugural Addresses of the American Presidents* (NY: Holt, Rinehart and Winston, 1961), p. 86. Charles E. Rice, *The Supreme Court and Public Prayer* (New York: Fordham University Press, 1964), p. 182. Arthur Schlesinger Jr., ed., *The Chief Executive* (NY: Chelsea House Publishers, 1965), pp. 93-94. Stephen Abbott Northrop, D.D., *A Cloud of Witnesses* (Portland, Oregon: American Heritage Ministries, 1987; Mantle Ministries, 228 Still Ridge, Bulverde, Texas), p. 215. Peter Marshall and David Manuel, *The Glory of America* (Bloomington, MN: Garborg's Heart 'N Home, Inc., 1991), 4.4. J. Michael Sharman, J.D., *Faith of the Fathers* (Culpepper, Virginia: Victory Publishing, 1995), pp. 43-44.

[35] **William Henry Harrison.** March 4, 1841, Thursday, in his Inaugural Address. James D. Richardson (U.S. Representative from Tennessee), ed., *A Compilation of the Messages and Papers of the Presidents 1789-1897*, 10 vols. (Washington, D.C.: U.S. Government Printing Office, published by Authority of Congress, 1897, 1899; Washington, D.C.: Bureau of National Literature and Art, *1789-1902*, 11 vols., 1907, 1910), Vol. 4, pp. 6-20. Benjamin Franklin Morris, *The Christian Life and Character of the Civil Institutions of the United States* (Philadelphia: George W. Childs, 1864), p. 605. *Inaugural Addresses of the Presidents of the United States - From George Washington 1789 to Richard Milhous Nixon 1969* (Washington, D.C.: United States Government Printing Office; 91st Congress, 1st Session, House Document 91-142, 1969), pp. 71-87. Davis Newton Lott, *The Inaugural Addresses of the American Presidents* (NY: Holt, Rinehart and Winston, 1961), p. 86. Charles E. Rice, *The Supreme Court and Public Prayer* (New York: Fordham University Press, 1964), p. 182. Arthur Schlesinger Jr., ed., *The Chief Executive* (NY: Chelsea House Publishers, 1965), pp. 93-94. Stephen Abbott Northrop, D.D., *A Cloud of Witnesses* (Portland, Oregon: American Heritage Ministries, 1987; Mantle Ministries, 228 Still Ridge, Bulverde, Texas), p. 215. Peter Marshall and David Manuel, *The Glory of America* (Bloomington, MN: Garborg's Heart 'N Home, Inc., 1991), 4.4. J. Michael Sharman, J.D., *Faith of the Fathers* (Culpepper, Virginia: Victory Publishing, 1995), pp. 43-44.

[36] **William Henry Harrison.** March 4, 1841, Thursday, in his Inaugural Address. James D. Richardson (U.S. Representative from Tennessee), ed., *A Compilation of the Messages and Papers of the Presidents 1789-1897*, 10 vols. (Washington, D.C.: U.S. Government Printing Office, published by Authority of Congress, 1897, 1899; Washington, D.C.: Bureau of National Literature and Art, *1789-1902*, 11 vols., 1907, 1910), Vol. 4, pp. 6-20. Benjamin Franklin Morris, *The Christian Life and Character of the Civil Institutions of the United States* (Philadelphia: George W. Childs, 1864), p. 605. *Inaugural Addresses of the Presidents of the United States - From George Washington 1789 to Richard Milhous Nixon 1969* (Washington, D.C.: United States Government Printing Office; 91st Congress, 1st Session, House Document 91-142, 1969), pp. 71-87. Davis Newton Lott, *The Inaugural Addresses of the American Presidents* (NY: Holt, Rinehart and Winston, 1961), p. 86. Charles E. Rice, *The Supreme Court and Public Prayer* (New York: Fordham University Press, 1964), p. 182. Arthur Schlesinger Jr., ed., *The Chief Executive* (NY: Chelsea House Publishers, 1965), pp. 93-94. Stephen Abbott Northrop, D.D., *A Cloud of Witnesses* (Portland, Oregon: American Heritage Ministries, 1987; Mantle Ministries, 228 Still Ridge, Bulverde, Texas), p. 215. Peter Marshall and David Manuel, *The Glory of America* (Bloomington, MN: Garborg's Heart 'N Home, Inc., 1991), 4.4. J. Michael Sharman, J.D., *Faith of the Fathers* (Culpepper, Virginia: Victory Publishing, 1995), pp. 43-44.

[37] **John Tyler.** April 9, 1841, in his Inaugural Address delivered in Washington, D.C. James D. Richardson (U.S. Representative from Tennessee), ed., *A Compilation of the Messages and Papers of the Presidents 1789-1897*, 10 vols. (Washington, D.C.: U.S. Government Printing Office, published by Authority of Congress, 1897, 1899; Washington, D.C.: Bureau of National Literature and Art, *1789-1902*, 11 vols., 1907, 1910), Vol. IV, pp. 36-39.

[38] **John Tyler.** April 13, 1841, in a Proclamation recommending a National Day of Fasting and Prayer in respect of the death of President William Henry Harrison, issued from Washington, D.C. James D. Richardson (U.S. Representative from Tennessee), ed., *A Compilation of the Messages and Papers of the Presidents 1789-1897*, 10 vols. (Washington, D.C.: U.S. Government Printing Office, published by Authority of Congress, 1897, 1899; Washington, D.C.: Bureau of National Literature and Art, *1789-1902*, 11 vols., 1907, 1910), Vol. IV, p. 32. Benjamin Franklin Morris, *The Christian Life and Character of the Civil Institutions of the United States* (Philadelphia: George W. Childs, 1864), pp. 550-551.

[39] **John Tyler.** December 6, 1842, in his Second Annual Message to the Senate and House of Representatives of the United States. James D. Richardson (U.S.

Representative from Tennessee), ed., *A Compilation of the Messages and Papers of the Presidents 1789-1897*, 10 vols. (Washington, D.C.: U.S. Government Printing Office, published by Authority of Congress, 1897, 1899; Washington, D.C.: Bureau of National Literature and Art, *1789-1902*, 11 vols., 1907, 1910), Vol. IV, pp. 194, 199.

[40] **John Tyler.** December 3, 1844, in his Fourth Annual Message to Congress. James D. Richardson (U.S. Representative from Tennessee), ed., *A Compilation of the Messages and Papers of the Presidents 1789-1897*, 10 vols. (Washington, D.C.: U.S. Government Printing Office, published by Authority of Congress, 1897, 1899; Washington, D.C.: Bureau of National Literature and Art, *1789-1902*, 11 vols., 1907, 1910), Vol. IV, pp. 334-336.

[41] **James Knox Polk.** March 4, 1845, Tuesday, in his Inaugural Address. James D. Richardson (U.S. Representative from Tennessee), ed., *A Compilation of the Messages and Papers of the Presidents 1789-1897*, 10 vols. (Washington, D.C.: U.S. Government Printing Office, published by Authority of Congress, 1897, 1899; Washington, D.C.: Bureau of National Literature and Art, *1789-1902*, 11 vols., 1907, 1910), Vol. 4, pp. 373-382. Benjamin Franklin Morris, *The Christian Life and Character of the Civil Institutions of the United States* (Philadelphia: George W. Childs, 1864), p. 607. *Inaugural Addresses of the Presidents*, House Document #540, 1952, p. 90. *Inaugural Addresses of the Presidents of the United States - From George Washington 1789 to Richard Milhous Nixon 1969* (Washington, D.C.: United States Government Printing Office; 91st Congress, 1st Session, House Document 91-142, 1969), pp. 89-98. Arthur Schlesinger Jr., ed., *The Chief Executive* (NY: Chelsea House Publishers, 1965), p. 106. Charles E. Rice, *The Supreme Court and Public Prayer* (New York: Fordham University Press, 1964), pp. 182-183. Benjamin Weiss, *God in American History: A Documentation of America's Religious Heritage* (Grand Rapids, MI: Zondervan, 1966), p. 80. Willard Cantelon, *Money Master of the World* (Plainfield, NJ: Logos International, 1976), p. 190. Peter Marshall and David Manuel, *The Glory of America* (Bloomington, MN: Garborg's Heart 'N Home, Inc., 1991), 4.6. J. Michael Sharman, J.D., *Faith of the Fathers* (Culpepper, Virginia: Victory Publishing, 1995), pp. 47-48.

[42] **James Knox Polk.** June 16, 1845, directed George Bancroft, Acting Secretary of War and Secretary of the Navy, to issued the General Order, No. 27, from the War Department, Adjutant-General R. Jones' Office, announcing Andrew Jackson's death. James D. Richardson (U.S. Representative from Tennessee), ed., *A Compilation of the Messages and Papers of the Presidents 1789-1897*, 10 vols. (Washington, D.C.: U.S. Government Printing Office, published by Authority of Congress, 1897, 1899; Washington, D.C.: Bureau of National Literature and Art, *1789-1902*, 11 vols., 1907, 1910), Vol. 4, pp. 384-385.

[43] **James Know Polk.** December 2, 1845, in his First Annual Message to Congress. James D. Richardson (U.S. Representative from Tennessee), ed., *A Compilation of the Messages and Papers of the Presidents 1789-1897*, 10 vols. (Washington, D.C.: U.S. Government Printing Office, published by Authority of Congress, 1897, 1899; Washington, D.C.: Bureau of National Literature and Art, *1789-1902*, 11 vols., 1907, 1910), Vol. 4, pp. 385-386, 407-408, 416.

[44] **James Knox Polk.** December 7, 1847, in his Third Annual Message to Congress. James D. Richardson (U.S. Representative from Tennessee), ed., *A Compilation of the Messages and Papers of the Presidents 1789-1897*, 10 vols. (Washington, D.C.: U.S. Government Printing Office, published by Authority of Congress, 1897, 1899; Washington, D.C.: Bureau of National Literature and Art, *1789-1902*, 11 vols., 1907, 1910), Vol. 4, pp. 532-533, 564. Benjamin Franklin Morris, *The Christian Life and Character of the Civil Institutions of the United States* (Philadelphia: George W. Childs, 1864), p. 607.

[45] **Zachary Taylor.** March 5, 1849, Monday, in his Inaugural Address, which he moved from March 4, Sunday, as he refused to be sworn in on the Sabbath. James D. Richardson (U.S. Representative from Tennessee), ed., *A Compilation of the Messages and Papers of the Presidents 1789-1897*, 10 vols. (Washington, D.C.: U.S. Government Printing Office, published by Authority of Congress, 1897, 1899; Washington, D.C.: Bureau of National Literature and Art, *1789-1902*, 11 vols., 1907, 1910), Vol. 5, pp. 5-6. Benjamin Franklin Morris, *The Christian Life and Character of the Civil Institutions of the United States* (Philadelphia: George W. Childs, 1864), p. 607. *Inaugural Addresses of the Presidents of the United States - From George Washington 1789 to Richard Milhous Nixon 1969* (Washington, D.C.: United States Government Printing Office; 91st Congress, 1st Session, House Document 91-142, 1969), pp. 99-101. Davis Newton Lott, *The Inaugural Addresses of the American Presidents* (NY: Holt, Rinehart and Winston, 1961), p. 100. Charles E. Rice, *The Supreme Court and Public Prayer* (New York: Fordham University Press, 1964), p. 183. J. Michael Sharman, J.D., *Faith of the Fathers* (Culpepper, Virginia: Victory Publishing, 1995), p. 50.

[46] **Zachary Taylor.** August 4, 1849, Friday, in Proclamation of a National Day of Prayer as an epidemic of cholera had begun to plague the nation. Benjamin Franklin Morris, *The Christian Life and Character of the Civil Institutions of the United States* (Philadelphia: George W. Childs, 1864), pp. 551-552. Benjamin Franklin Morris, *The*

Christian Life and Character of the Civil Institutions of the United States (Philadelphia: George W. Childs, 1864), p. 608. Gary DeMar, "Does Anyone Have a Prayer?" (Atlanta, GA: *The Biblical Worldview*, An American Vision Publication - American Vision, Inc.), p. 2.

[47] **Zachary Taylor.** July 4, 1849, at a Sabbath-school celebration in the city of Washington. Benjamin Franklin Morris, *The Christian Life and Character of the Civil Institutions of the United States* (Philadelphia: George W. Childs, 1864), p. 608.

[48] **Zachary Taylor.** December 4, 1849, in his First Annual Message to Congress. James D. Richardson (U.S. Representative from Tennessee), ed., *A Compilation of the Messages and Papers of the Presidents 1789-1897*, 10 vols. (Washington, D.C.: U.S. Government Printing Office, published by Authority of Congress, 1897, 1899; Washington, D.C.: Bureau of National Literature and Art, *1789-1902*, 11 vols., 1907, 1910), Vol. 5, pp. 9-10, 24. Benjamin Franklin Morris, *The Christian Life and Character of the Civil Institutions of the United States* (Philadelphia: George W. Childs, 1864), p. 608.

[49] **Millard Fillmore.** July 10, 1850, in an address to Congress after assuming the Presidency the day after President Zachary Taylor died. James D. Richardson (U.S. Representative from Tennessee), ed., *A Compilation of the Messages and Papers of the Presidents 1789-1897*, 10 vols. (Washington, D.C.: U.S. Government Printing Office, published by Authority of Congress, 1897, 1899; Washington, D.C.: Bureau of National Literature and Art, *1789-1902*, 11 vols., 1907, 1910), Vol. 5, p. 64.

[50] **Millard Fillmore.** December 2, 1850, in his First Annual Message to Congress. James D. Richardson (U.S. Representative from Tennessee), ed., *A Compilation of the Messages and Papers of the Presidents 1789-1897*, 10 vols. (Washington, D.C.: U.S. Government Printing Office, published by Authority of Congress, 1897, 1899; Washington, D.C.: Bureau of National Literature and Art, *1789-1902*, 11 vols., 1907, 1910), Vol. 5, pp. 77-78, 93-94. Benjamin Franklin Morris, *The Christian Life and Character of the Civil Institutions of the United States* (Philadelphia: George W. Childs, 1864), p. 608.

[51] **Millard Fillmore.** December 2, 1851, in his Second Annual Message to Congress. James D. Richardson (U.S. Representative from Tennessee), ed., *A Compilation of the Messages and Papers of the Presidents 1789-1897*, 10 vols. (Washington, D.C.: U.S. Government Printing Office, published by Authority of Congress, 1897, 1899; Washington, D.C.: Bureau of National Literature and Art, *1789-1902*, 11 vols., 1907, 1910), Vol. 5, p. 113. Benjamin Franklin Morris, *The Christian Life and Character of the Civil Institutions of the United States* (Philadelphia: George W. Childs, 1864), p. 609.

[52] **Millard Fillmore.** December 6, 1852, in his Third Annual Message to Congress. James D. Richardson (U.S. Representative from Tennessee), ed., *A Compilation of the Messages and Papers of the Presidents 1789-1897*, 10 vols. (Washington, D.C.: U.S. Government Printing Office, published by Authority of Congress, 1897, 1899; Washington, D.C.: Bureau of National Literature and Art, *1789-1902*, 11 vols., 1907, 1910), Vol. 5, pp. 163, 179-182. Benjamin Franklin Morris, *The Christian Life and Character of the Civil Institutions of the United States* (Philadelphia: George W. Childs, 1864), p. 609.

[53] **Franklin Pierce.** March 4, 1853, in his Inaugural Address delivered from the steps of the Capitol building. James D. Richardson (U.S. Representative from Tennessee), ed., *A Compilation of the Messages and Papers of the Presidents 1789-1897*, 10 vols. (Washington, D.C.: U.S. Government Printing Office, published by Authority of Congress, 1897, 1899; Washington, D.C.: Bureau of National Literature and Art, *1789-1902*, 11 vols., 1907, 1910), Vol. 5, pp. 197-203. Benjamin Franklin Morris, *The Christian Life and Character of the Civil Institutions of the United States* (Philadelphia: George W. Childs, 1864), p. 609. *Inaugural Addresses of the Presidents of the United States - From George Washington 1789 to Richard Milhous Nixon 1969* (Washington, D.C.: United States Government Printing Office; 91st Congress, 1st Session, House Document 91-142, 1969), pp. 103-109. Davis Newton Lott, *The Inaugural Addresses of the American Presidents* (NY: Holt, Rinehart and Winston, 1961), pp. 104, 107, 108. Charles E. Rice, *The Supreme Court and Public Prayer* (New York: Fordham University Press, 1964), pp. 183-184. Arthur Schlesinger, ed., *The Chief Executive* (NY: Chelsea House Publishers, 1965), pp. 113-114, 117, 118. Benjamin Weiss, *God in American History: A Documentation of America's Religious Heritage* (Grand Rapids, MI: Zondervan, 1966), p. 86. Willard Cantelon, *Money Master of the World* (Plainfield, NJ: Logos International, 1976), p. 120. J. Michael Sharman, J.D., *Faith of the Fathers* (Culpepper, Virginia: Victory Publishing, 1995), pp. 53-54.

[54] **Franklin Pierce.** December 5, 1853, in his First Annual Message to Congress. James D. Richardson (U.S. Representative from Tennessee), ed., *A Compilation of the Messages and Papers of the Presidents 1789-1897*, 10 vols. (Washington, D.C.: U.S. Government Printing Office, published by Authority of Congress, 1897, 1899; Washington, D.C.: Bureau of National Literature and Art, *1789-1902*, 11 vols., 1907, 1910), Vol. 5, pp. 207, 213. Benjamin Franklin Morris, *The Christian Life and Character of the Civil Institutions of the United States* (Philadelphia: George W. Childs, 1864), pp. 609-610. Stephen Abbott Northrop, D.D., *A Cloud of Witnesses*

(Portland, OR: American Heritage Ministries, 1987; Mantle Ministries, 228 Still Ridge, Bulverde, Texas), p. 361.

[55] **Franklin Pierce.** December 4, 1854, in his Second Annual Message. James D. Richardson (U.S. Representative from Tennessee), ed., *A Compilation of the Messages and Papers of the Presidents 1789-1897*, 10 vols. (Washington, D.C.: U.S. Government Printing Office, published by Authority of Congress, 1897, 1899; Washington, D.C.: Bureau of National Literature and Art, *1789-1902*, 11 vols., 1907, 1910), Vol. 5, pp. 273, 292-293.

[56] **Franklin Pierce.** January 16, 1857, in communication to the Senate. James D. Richardson (U.S. Representative from Tennessee), ed., *A Compilation of the Messages and Papers of the Presidents 1789-1897*, 10 vols. (Washington, D.C.: U.S. Government Printing Office, published by Authority of Congress, 1897, 1899; Washington, D.C.: Bureau of National Literature and Art, *1789-1902*, 11 vols., 1907, 1910), Vol. 5, p. 420.

[57] **James Buchanan.** March 4, 1857, Wednesday, in his Inaugural Address. James D. Richardson (U.S. Representative from Tennessee), ed., *A Compilation of the Messages and Papers of the Presidents 1789-1897*, 10 vols. (Washington, D.C.: U.S. Government Printing Office, published by Authority of Congress, 1897, 1899; Washington, D.C.: Bureau of National Literature and Art, *1789-1902*, 11 vols., 1907, 1910), Vol. 5, pp. 431-436. *Inaugural Addresses of the Presidents of the United States - From George Washington 1789 to Richard Milhous Nixon 1969* (Washington, D.C.: United States Government Printing Office; 91st Congress, 1st Session, House Document 91-142, 1969), pp. 111-117. Benjamin Franklin Morris, *The Christian Life and Character of the Civil Institutions of the United States* (Philadelphia: George W. Childs, 1864), p. 610. Davis Newton Lott, ed., *The Inaugural Addresses of the American Presidents* (NY: Holt, Rinehart and Winston, 1961), pp. 111, 115. Charles E. Rice, *The Supreme Court and Public Prayer* (New York: Fordham University Press, 1964), p. 184. Arthur Schlesinger, ed., *The Chief Executive* (NY: Chelsea House Publishers, 1965), pp. 121, 126. J. Michael Sharman, J.D., *Faith of the Fathers* (Culpepper, Virginia: Victory Publishing, 1995), p. 56.

[58] **James Buchanan.** December 19, 1859, in his Third Annual Message to Congress. James D. Richardson (U.S. Representative from Tennessee), ed., *A Compilation of the Messages and Papers of the Presidents 1789-1897*, 10 vols. (Washington, D.C.: U.S. Government Printing Office, published by Authority of Congress, 1897, 1899; Washington, D.C.: Bureau of National Literature and Art, *1789-1902*, 11 vols., 1907, 1910), Vol. 5, pp. 552-558.

[59] **James Buchanan.** December 3, 1860, in his Fourth Annual Message to Congress. James D. Richardson (U.S. Representative from Tennessee), ed., *A Compilation of the Messages and Papers of the Presidents 1789-1897*, 10 vols. (Washington, D.C.: U.S. Government Printing Office, published by Authority of Congress, 1897, 1899; Washington, D.C.: Bureau of National Literature and Art, *1789-1902*, 11 vols., 1907, 1910), Vol. 5, pp. 627-649.

[60] **James Buchanan.** December 14, 1860, in a Proclamation of a National Day of Humiliation, Fasting, and Prayer. James D. Richardson (U.S. Representative from Tennessee), ed., *A Compilation of the Messages and Papers of the Presidents 1789-1897*, 10 vols. (Washington, D.C.: U.S. Government Printing Office, published by Authority of Congress, 1897, 1899; Washington, D.C.: Bureau of National Literature and Art, *1789-1902*, 11 vols., , 1907, 1910), Vol. X, pp. 79-80. Benjamin Franklin Morris, *The Christian Life and Character of the Civil Institutions of the United States* (Philadelphia: George W. Childs, 1864), pp. 555-556.

[61] **Abraham Lincoln.** March 4, 1861, Monday, in his First Inaugural Address. James D. Richardson (U.S. Representative from Tennessee), ed., *A Compilation of the Messages and Papers of the Presidents 1789-1897*, 10 vols. (Washington, D.C.: U.S. Government Printing Office, published by Authority of Congress, 1897, 1899; Washington, D.C.: Bureau of National Literature and Art, *1789-1902*, 11 vols., 1907, 1910), Vol. VI, pp. 9-11. *Inaugural Addresses of the Presidents of the United States - From George Washington 1789 to Richard Milhous Nixon 1969* (Washington, D.C.: United States Government Printing Office; 91st Congress, 1st Session, House Document 91-142, 1969), pp. 119-126. Benjamin Franklin Morris, *The Christian Life and Character of the Civil Institutions of the United States* (Philadelphia: George W. Childs, 1864), p. 611. Charles W. Eliot, LL.D., ed., *American Historical Documents 1000-1904* (New York: P.F. Collier & Son Company, *The Harvard Classics*, 1910), Vol. 43, pp. 334-343. Albert J. Beveridge, *The Life of John Marshall* (Boston: Houghton Mifflin, 1919), Vol. VI, p. 9. Roy P. Basler, ed., *The Collected Works of Abraham Lincoln*, 9 vols. (New Brunswick, NJ: Rutgers University Press, 1953), Vol. IV, p. 271. Paul M. Angle, ed., *By These Words* (NY: Rand McNally & Company, 1954), p. 224. Davis Newton Lott, *The Inaugural Addresses of the American Presidents* (NY: Holt, Rinehart and Winston, 1961), p. 122. Richard D. Heffner, *A Documentary History of the United States* (New York: The New American Library of World Literature, Inc., 1961), pp. 144-146. Charles E. Rice, *The Supreme Court and Public Prayer* (New York: Fordham University Press, 1964), p. 184. David Barton, *The Myth of Separation* (Aledo, TX: WallBuilder Press, 1991), p. 242. Mark A. Knoll, *The Puzzling Faith of Abraham Lincoln* (Carol Stream, IL: Christian History), Vol. XI, No. 1, Issue 33, p. 11. William McKinley, July 4, 1892, while serving as Governor of Ohio, quoted Lincoln

in an address to the Baptist Young People's Union in Lakeside, Ohio. Stephen Abbott Northrop, D.D., *A Cloud of Witnesses* (Portland, OR: American Heritage Ministries, 1987; Mantle Ministries, 228 Still Ridge, Bulverde, Texas), p. 313. William Safire, ed., *Lend Me Your Ears - Great Speeches in History* (NY: W.W. Norton & Company 1992), p. 746. J. Michael Sharman, J.D., *Faith of the Fathers* (Culpepper, Virginia: Victory Publishing, 1995), p. 58.

[62] **Abraham Lincoln.** August 12, 1861, in a Proclamation of a *National Day of Humiliation, Prayer, and Fasting,* issued after the Union army was defeated at the *Battle of Bull Run.* James D. Richardson (U.S. Representative from Tennessee), ed., *A Compilation of the Messages and Papers of the Presidents 1789-1897,* 10 vols. (Washington, D.C.: U.S. Government Printing Office, published by Authority of Congress, 1897, 1899; Washington, D.C.: Bureau of National Literature and Art, *1789-1902,* 11 vols., 1907, 1910), Vol. VI, pp. 36-37. Benjamin Franklin Morris, *The Christian Life and Character of the Civil Institutions of the United States* (Philadelphia: George W. Childs, 1864), p. 557. William J. Johnson, *Abraham Lincoln, The Christian* (NY: The Abington Press, 1913), p. 76. Trueblood, *Abraham Lincoln: Theologian of American Anguish,* pp. 76-86. Peter Marshall and David Manuel, *The Glory of America* (Bloomington, MN: Garborg's Heart'N Home, Inc., 1991), 9.26, 8:12.

[63] **Abraham Lincoln.** March 30, 1863, in a Proclamation of a National Day of Humiliation, Fasting and Prayer. James D. Richardson (U.S. Representative from Tennessee), ed., *A Compilation of the Messages and Papers of the Presidents 1789-1897,* 10 vols. (Washington, D.C.: U.S. Government Printing Office, published by Authority of Congress, 1897, 1899; Washington, D.C.: Bureau of National Literature and Art, *1789-1902,* 11 vols., 1907, 1910), Vol. VI, pp. 164-165. Benjamin Franklin Morris, *The Christian Life and Character of the Civil Institutions of the United States* (Philadelphia: George W. Childs, 1864), pp. 558-559. Roy P. Basler, ed., *The Collected Works of Abraham Lincoln,* 9 vols. (New Brunswick, NJ: Rutgers University Press, 1953), Vol. 6, p. 179. Benjamin Weiss, *God in American History: A Documentation of America's Religious Heritage* (Grand Rapids, MI: Zondervan, 1966), p. 92. Willard Cantelon, *Money Master of the World* (Plainfield, NJ: Logos International, 1976), p. 120. Gary DeMar, *God and Government, A Biblical and Historical Study* (Atlanta, GA: American Vision Press, 1984), pp. 128-29. David Barton, *The Myth of Separation* (Aledo, TX: WallBuilder Press, 1991), p. 259. "Our Christian Heritage," *Letter from Plymouth Rock* (Marlborough, NH: The Plymouth Rock Foundation), p. 6. D.P. Diffine, Ph.D., *One Nation Under God - How Close a Separation?* (Searcy, Arkansas: Harding University, Belden Center for Private Enterprise Education, 6th edition, 1992), pp. 14-15. Gary DeMar, *America's Christian History: The Untold Story* (Atlanta, GA: American Vision Publishers, Inc., 1993), pp. 53, 99.

[64] **Abraham Lincoln.** March 4, 1865, Saturday, in his Second Inaugural Address. Abraham Lincoln, *Second Inaugural Address-1865* (Washington, D.C.: Lincoln Memorial, inscribed on the North Wall). James D. Richardson (U.S. Representative from Tennessee), ed., *A Compilation of the Messages and Papers of the Presidents 1789-1897,* 10 vols. (Washington, D.C.: U.S. Government Printing Office, published by Authority of Congress, 1897, 1899; Washington, D.C.: Bureau of National Literature and Art, *1789-1902,* 11 vols., 1907, 1910), Vol. VI, pp. 276-277. *Inaugural Addresses of the Presidents of the United States - From George Washington 1789 to Richard Milhous Nixon 1969* (Washington, D.C.: United States Government Printing Office, 91st Congress, 1st Session, House Document 91-142, 1969), pp. 127-128. John G. Nicolay and John Hay, eds., *The Complete Works of Abraham Lincoln: Speeches, Letters and State Papers* (1905), Vol. VIII, p. 333. Charles W. Eliot, LL.D., ed., *American Historical Documents 1000-1904* (New York: P.F. Collier & Son Company, *The Harvard Classics,* 1910), Vol. 43, pp. 450-452. Henry Steele Commager, ed., *Documents of American History,* 2 vols. (NY: F.S. Crofts and Company, 1934; Appleton-Century-Crofts, Inc., 1948, 6th edition, 1958; Englewood Cliffs, NJ: Prentice Hall, Inc., 9th edition, 1973), p. 443. Frederick C. Packard, Jr., ed., *Are You an American? - Great Americans Speak* (NY: Charles Scribner's Sons, 1951), p. 36. Roy Basler, ed., *Collected Works of Abraham Lincoln* (Rutgers University Press, 1953), Vol. VIII p. 33. Richard D. Heffner, *A Documentary History of the United States* (New York: The New American Library of World Literature, Inc., 1961), pp. 156-157. Charles E. Rice, *The Supreme Court and Public Prayer* (New York: Fordham University Press, 1964), pp. 184-185. Davis Newton Lott, *The Inaugural Addresses of the American Presidents* (NY: Holt, Rinehart and Winston, 1961), p. 126. Edmund Fuller and David E. Green, *God in the White House - The Faiths of American Presidents* (NY: Crown Publishers, Inc., 1968), p. 114. *The Annals of America,* 20 vols. (Chicago, IL: Encyclopedia Britannica, 1968), Vol. 9, p. 556. Lillian W. Kay, ed., *The Ground on Which We Stand - Basic Documents of American History* (NY: Franklin Watts., Inc, 1969), p. 201. Vincent J. Wilson, ed., *The Book of Great American Documents* (Brookfield, MD: American History Research Associates, 1987), p. 80. Ronald Reid, ed., *Three Centuries of American Rhetorical Discourse - An Anthology and a Review* (Prospect Heights, Ill: Waveland Press, Inc., 1988), p. 466. Mark A. Knoll, *The Puzzling Faith of Abraham Lincoln* (Carol Stream, IL: Christian History), Vol. XI, No. 1, Issue 33, p. 12. Peter Marshall and David Manuel, *The Glory of America* (Bloomington, MN: Garborg's Heart'N Home, Inc., 1991), 3.4. Catherine Millard, *The Rewriting of America's History* (Camp Hill, PA: Horizon House Publishers, 1991),

pp. 168-169. Michael Barone, "Who Was Lincoln?" *U.S. News & World Report* (October 5, 1992), p. 71. William Safire, ed., *Lend Me Your Ears - Great Speeches in History* (NY: W.W. Norton & Company 1992), p. 441. Gary DeMar, *America's Christian History: The Untold Story* (Atlanta, GA: American Vision Publishers, Inc., 1993), p. 99. J. Michael Sharman, J.D., *Faith of the Fathers* (Culpepper, Virginia: Victory Publishing, 1995), p. 59-60.

[65] **Andrew Johnson.** April 25, 1865, in a Proclamation of a National Day of Humiliation and Mourning. James D. Richardson (U.S. Representative from Tennessee), ed., *A Compilation of the Messages and Papers of the Presidents 1789-1897*, 10 vols. (Washington, D.C.: U.S. Government Printing Office, published by Authority of Congress, 1897, 1899; Washington, D.C.: Bureau of National Literature and Art, *1789-1902*, 11 vols., 1907, 1910), Vol. VI, p. 306.

[66] **Andrew Johnson.** October 8, 1866, in a Proclamation of a *National Day of Thanksgiving and Praise*. James D. Richardson (U.S. Representative from Tennessee), ed., *A Compilation of the Messages and Papers of the Presidents 1789-1897*, 10 vols. (Washington, D.C.: U.S. Government Printing Office, published by Authority of Congress, 1897, 1899; Washington, D.C.: Bureau of National Literature and Art, *1789-1902*, 11 vols., 1907, 1910), Vol. VI, pp. 438-439.

[67] **Andrew Johnson.** September 7, 1867; May 29, 1865, in Proclamations of Amnesty and Pardon to the participants of the Confederate insurrection; also December 8, 1863, March 26, 1864 in Proclamations of Amnesty and Pardon issued by President Abraham Lincoln. James D. Richardson (U.S. Representative from Tennessee), ed., *A Compilation of the Messages and Papers of the Presidents 1789-1897*, 10 vols. (Washington, D.C.: U.S. Government Printing Office, published by Authority of Congress, 1897, 1899; Washington, D.C.: Bureau of National Literature and Art, *1789-1902*, 11 vols., 1907, 1910), Vol. VI, pp. 213-215, 310-311, 548-549. Charles W. Eliot, LL.D., ed., *American Historical Documents 1000-1904* (New York: P.F. Collier & Son Company, *The Harvard Classics*, 1910), Vol. 43, p. 443.

[68] **Andrew Johnson.** December 3, 1867, in his Third Annual Message. James D. Richardson (U.S. Representative from Tennessee), ed., *A Compilation of the Messages and Papers of the Presidents 1789-1897*, 10 vols. (Washington, D.C.: U.S. Government Printing Office, published by Authority of Congress, 1897, 1899; Washington, D.C.: Bureau of National Literature and Art, *1789-1902*, 11 vols., 1907, 1910), Vol. VI, pp. 559-563.

[69] **Ulysses Simpson Grant.** March 4, 1869, Thursday, in his First Inaugural Address. James D. Richardson (U.S. Representative from Tennessee), ed., *A Compilation of the Messages and Papers of the Presidents 1789-1897*, 10 vols. (Washington, D.C.: U.S. Government Printing Office, published by Authority of Congress, 1897, 1899; Washington, D.C.: Bureau of National Literature and Art, *1789-1902*, 11 vols., 1907, 1910), Vol. 7, pp. 7-8. *Inaugural Addresses of the Presidents of the United States - From George Washington 1789 to Richard Milhous Nixon 1969* (Washington, D.C.: United States Government Printing Office; 91st Congress, 1st Session, House Document 91-142, 1969), pp. 129-131. Davis Newton Lott, ed., *The Inaugural Addresses of the American Presidents* (NY: Holt, Rinehart and Winston, 1961), p. 131. Charles E. Rice, *The Supreme Court and Public Prayer* (New York: Fordham University Press, 1964), p. 185. Arthur Schlesinger, Jr., ed., *The Chief Executive* (NY: Chelsea House Publishers, 1965), p. 144. J. Michael Sharman, J.D., *Faith of the Fathers* (Culpepper, Virginia: Victory Publishing, 1995), p. 63.

[70] **Ulysses Simpson Grant.** December 5, 1870, Monday, in his Second Annual Message to Congress. James D. Richardson (U.S. Representative from Tennessee), ed., *A Compilation of the Messages and Papers of the Presidents 1789-1897*, 10 vols. (Washington, D.C.: U.S. Government Printing Office, published by Authority of Congress, 1897, 1899; Washington, D.C.: Bureau of National Literature and Art, *1789-1902*, 11 vols., 1907, 1910), Vol. 7, pp. 109-110.

[71] **Ulysses Simpson Grant.** March 4, 1873, Tuesday, in his Second Inaugural Address. James D. Richardson (U.S. Representative from Tennessee), ed., *A Compilation of the Messages and Papers of the Presidents 1789-1897*, 10 vols. (Washington, D.C.: U.S. Government Printing Office, published by Authority of Congress, 1897, 1899; Washington, D.C.: Bureau of National Literature and Art, *1789-1902*, 11 vols., 1907, 1910), Vol. 7, pp. 221-222. *Inaugural Addresses of the Presidents of the United States - From George Washington 1789 to Richard Milhous Nixon 1969* (Washington, D.C.: United States Government Printing Office; 91st Congress, 1st Session, House Document 91-142, 1969), pp. 132-134. Davis Newton Lott, ed., *The Inaugural Addresses of the American Presidents* (NY: Holt, Rinehart and Winston, 1961), p. 133. Charles E. Rice, *The Supreme Court and Public Prayer* (New York: Fordham University Press, 1964), pp. 185-186. Arthur Schlesinger Jr., ed., *The Chief Executive* (NY: Chelsea House Publishers, 1965), pp. 145, 147. J. Michael Sharman, J.D., *Faith of the Fathers* (Culpepper, Virginia: Victory Publishing, 1995), p. 64.

[72] **Ulysses Simpson Grant.** October 27, 1875, in a Proclamation of a *National Day of Thanksgiving*. James D. Richardson (U.S. Representative from Tennessee), ed., *A Compilation of the Messages and Papers of the Presidents 1789-1897*, 10 vols. (Washington, D.C.: U.S. Government Printing Office, published by Authority of Congress, 1897, 1899; Washington, D.C.: Bureau of National Literature and Art, *1789-1902*, 11 vols., 1907, 1910), Vol. 7, pp. 325-326.

[73] **Rutherford Birchard Hayes.** March 5, 1877, Monday, in his Inaugural Address. James D. Richardson (U.S. Representative from Tennessee), ed., *A Compilation of the Messages and Papers of the Presidents 1789-1897*, 10 vols. (Washington, D.C.: U.S. Government Printing Office, published by Authority of Congress, 1897, 1899; Washington, D.C.: Bureau of National Literature and Art, *1789-1902*, 11 vols., 1907, 1910), Vol. 7, pp. 446-447. *Inaugural Addresses of the Presidents of the United States - From George Washington 1789 to Richard Milhous Nixon 1969* (Washington, D.C.: United States Government Printing Office; 91st Congress, 1st Session, House Document 91-142, 1969), pp. 135-140. Davis Newton Lott, *The Inaugural Addresses of the American Presidents* (NY: Holt, Rinehart and Winston, 1961), p. 141. Charles E. Rice, *The Supreme Court and Public Prayer* (New York: Fordham University Press, 1964), p. 186. Arthur Schlesinger Jr., ed., *The Chief Executive* (NY: Chelsea House Publishers, 1965), p. 155. Benjamin Weiss, *God in American History: A Documentation of America's Religious Heritage* (Grand Rapids, MI: Zondervan, 1966), p. 103. Willard Cantelon, *Money Master of the World* (Plainfield, NJ: Logos International, 1976), p. 120. J. Michael Sharman, J.D., *Faith of the Fathers* (Culpepper, Virginia: Victory Publishing, 1995), pp. 66-67.

[74] **Rutherford Birchard Hayes.** December 3, 1877, in his First Annual Message. James D. Richardson (U.S. Representative from Tennessee), ed., *A Compilation of the Messages and Papers of the Presidents 1789-1897*, 10 vols. (Washington, D.C.: U.S. Government Printing Office, published by Authority of Congress, 1897, 1899; Washington, D.C.: Bureau of National Literature and Art, *1789-1902*, 11 vols., 1907, 1910), Vol. 7, pp. 458, 469.

[75] **Rutherford Birchard Hayes.** November 3, 1879, in a Proclamation of a *National Day of Thanksgiving and Prayer*. James D. Richardson (U.S. Representative from Tennessee), ed., *A Compilation of the Messages and Papers of the Presidents 1789-1897*, 10 vols. (Washington, D.C.: U.S. Government Printing Office, published by Authority of Congress, 1897, 1899; Washington, D.C.: Bureau of National Literature and Art, *1789-1902*, 11 vols., 1907, 1910), Vol. 7, p. 548.

[76] **Rutherford Birchard Hayes.** November 1, 1880, in a Proclamation of a *National Day of Thanksgiving*. James D. Richardson (U.S. Representative from Tennessee), ed., *A Compilation of the Messages and Papers of the Presidents 1789-1897*, 10 vols. (Washington, D.C.: U.S. Government Printing Office, published by Authority of Congress, 1897, 1899; Washington, D.C.: Bureau of National Literature and Art, *1789-1902*, 11 vols., 1907, 1910), Vol. 7, p. 599.

[77] **James Abram Garfield.** March 4, 1881, Friday, in his Inaugural Address. James D. Richardson (U.S. Representative from Tennessee), ed., *A Compilation of the Messages and Papers of the Presidents 1789-1897*, 10 vols. (Washington, D.C.: U.S. Government Printing Office, published by Authority of Congress, 1897, 1899; Washington, D.C.: Bureau of National Literature and Art, *1789-1902*, 11 vols., 1907, 1910), Vol. 8, pp. 6-12. *Inaugural Addresses of the Presidents of the United States - From George Washington 1789 to Richard Milhous Nixon 1969* (Washington, D.C.: United States Government Printing Office; 91st Congress, 1st Session, House Document 91-142, 1969), pp. 141-147. Davis Newton Lott, ed., *The Inaugural Addresses of the American Presidents* (NY: Holt, Rinehart and Winston, 1961), pp. 146, 147, 148. Charles E. Rice, *The Supreme Court and Public Prayer* (New York: Fordham University Press, 1964), p. 186. Arthur Schlesinger Jr., ed., *The Chief Executive* (NY: Chelsea House Publishers, 1965), pp. 159, 160, 163. J. Michael Sharman, J.D., *Faith of the Fathers* (Culpepper, Virginia: Victory Publishing, 1995), pp. 69-70.

[78] **James Abram Garfield.** April 15, 1865, at a speech in New York at Lincoln's assassination. John Bartlett, *Bartlett's Familiar Quotations* (Boston: Little, Brown and Company, 1855, 1980), p. 609. Edmund Fuller and David E. Green, *God in the White House - The Faiths of American Presidents* (NY: Crown Publishers, Inc., 1968), p. 144.

[79] **James Abram Garfield.** 1876, in a speech commemorating the centennial of the Declaration of Independence. "A Century of Congress," by James A. Garfield, published in *Atlantic*, July 1877. John M. Taylor, *Garfield of Ohio - The Available Man* (NY: W.W. Norton and Company, Inc.), p. 180. David Barton, *The Myth of Separation*, (Aledo, TX: WallBuilder Press, 1991), p. 266. David Barton, *Keys to Good Government*, audio tape (Aledo, TX: WallBuilder Press, 1994).

[80] **James Abram Garfield.** September 20, 1881, Secretary of State James G. Blaine sent an announcement from Long Branch, N.J. to James Russell Lowell, U.S. Minister in London. James D. Richardson (U.S. Representative from Tennessee), ed., *A Compilation of the Messages and Papers of the Presidents 1789-1897*, 10 vols. (Washington, D.C.: U.S. Government Printing Office, published by Authority of Congress, 1897, 1899; Washington, D.C.: Bureau of National Literature and Art, *1789-1902*, 11 vols., 1907, 1910), Vol. 8, p. 15.

[81] **Chester Alan Arthur.** September 22, 1881, in a Proclamation of a National Day of Humiliation and Mourning. James D. Richardson (U.S. Representative from Tennessee), ed., *A Compilation of the Messages and Papers of the Presidents 1789-1897*, 10 vols. (Washington, D.C.: U.S. Government Printing Office, published by

Authority of Congress, 1897, 1899; Washington, D.C.: Bureau of National Literature and Art, *1789-1902,* 11 vols., 1907, 1910), Vol. VIII, p. 34.

[82] **Chester Alan Arthur.** November 4, 1881, in a Proclamation of a National Day of Thanksgiving and Prayer. James D. Richardson (U.S. Representative from Tennessee), ed., *A Compilation of the Messages and Papers of the Presidents 1789-1897,* 10 vols. (Washington, D.C.: U.S. Government Printing Office, published by Authority of Congress, 1897, 1899; Washington, D.C.: Bureau of National Literature and Art, *1789-1902,* 11 vols., 1907, 1910), Vol. 8, p. 36.

[83] **Chester Alan Arthur.** December 6, 1881, in his First Annual Message to Congress. James D. Richardson (U.S. Representative from Tennessee), ed., *A Compilation of the Messages and Papers of the Presidents 1789-1897,* 10 vols. (Washington, D.C.: U.S. Government Printing Office, published by Authority of Congress, 1897, 1899; Washington, D.C.: Bureau of National Literature and Art, *1789-1902,* 11 vols., 1907, 1910), Vol. 8, pp. 25-26, 37, 39, 40, 42, 57.

[84] **Chester Alan Arthur.** October 26, 1883, in a Proclamation of a National Day of Thanksgiving. James D. Richardson (U.S. Representative from Tennessee), ed., *A Compilation of the Messages and Papers of the Presidents 1789-1897,* 10 vols. (Washington, D.C.: U.S. Government Printing Office, published by Authority of Congress, 1897, 1899; Washington, D.C.: Bureau of National Literature and Art, *1789-1902,* 11 vols., 1907, 1910), Vol. 8, pp. 159-160.

[85] **(Stephen) Grover Cleveland.** March 4, 1885, Wednesday, in his First Inaugural Address. James D. Richardson (U.S. Representative from Tennessee), ed., *A Compilation of the Messages and Papers of the Presidents 1789-1897,* 10 vols. (Washington, D.C.: U.S. Government Printing Office, published by Authority of Congress, 1897, 1899; Washington, D.C.: Bureau of National Literature and Art, *1789-1902,* 11 vols., 1907, 1910), Vol. 8, pp. 300, 303. *Inaugural Addresses of the Presidents of the United States - From George Washington 1789 to Richard Milhous Nixon 1969* (Washington, D.C.: United States Government Printing Office; 91st Congress, 1st Session, House Document 91-142, 1969), pp. 149-152. Davis Newton Lott, *The Inaugural Addresses of the American Presidents* (NY: Holt, Rinehart and Winston, 1961), p. 142. Charles E. Rice, *The Supreme Court and Public Prayer* (New York: Fordham University Press, 1964), pp. 186-187. Benjamin Weiss, *God in American History - A Documentation of America's Religious Heritage* (Grand Rapids, MI: Zondervan, 1966), p. 109. Willard Cantelon, *Money Master of the World* (Plainfield, NJ: Logos International, 1976), p. 120. Peter Marshall and David Manuel, *The Glory of America* (Bloomington, MN: Garborg's Heart'N Home, Inc., 1991), 3.18. *Proclaim Liberty* (Dallas, TX: Word of Faith), p. 2. J. Michael Sharman, J.D., *Faith of the Fathers* (Culpepper, Virginia: Victory Publishing, 1995), p. 73.

[86] **(Stephen) Grover Cleveland.** November 2, 1885, in a Proclamation of a National Day of Thanksgiving and Prayer. James D. Richardson (U.S. Representative from Tennessee), ed., *A Compilation of the Messages and Papers of the Presidents 1789-1897,* 10 vols. (Washington, D.C.: U.S. Government Printing Office, published by Authority of Congress, 1897, 1899; Washington, D.C.: Bureau of National Literature and Art, *1789-1902,* 11 vols., 1907, 1910), Vol. 8, pp. 310-311.

[87] **(Stephen) Grover Cleveland.** December 8, 1885, in his First Annual Message to Congress. James D. Richardson (U.S. Representative from Tennessee), ed., *A Compilation of the Messages and Papers of the Presidents 1789-1897,* 10 vols. (Washington, D.C.: U.S. Government Printing Office, published by Authority of Congress, 1897, 1899; Washington, D.C.: Bureau of National Literature and Art, *1789-1902,* 11 vols., 1907, 1910), Vol. 8, pp. 361-362.

[88] **(Stephen) Grover Cleveland.** November 1, 1888, in a Proclamation of a National Day of Thanksgiving and Prayer. James D. Richardson (U.S. Representative from Tennessee), ed., *A Compilation of the Messages and Papers of the Presidents 1789-1897,* 10 vols. (Washington, D.C.: U.S. Government Printing Office, published by Authority of Congress, 1897, 1899; Washington, D.C.: Bureau of National Literature and Art, *1789-1902,* 11 vols., 1907, 1910), Vol. 8, pp. 743-744.

[89] **Benjamin Harrison.** March 4, 1889, in his Inaugural Address. James D. Richardson (U.S. Representative from Tennessee), ed., *A Compilation of the Messages and Papers of the Presidents 1789-1897,* 10 vols. (Washington, D.C.: U.S. Government Printing Office, published by Authority of Congress, 1897, 1899; Washington, D.C.: Bureau of National Literature and Art, *1789-1902,* 11 vols., 1907, 1910), Vol. IX, pp. 6-13. *Inaugural Addresses of the Presidents of the United States - From George Washington 1789 to Richard Milhous Nixon 1969* (Washington, D.C.: United States Government Printing Office; 91st Congress, 1st Session, House Document 91-142, 1969), pp. 153-162. Davis Newton Lott, *The Inaugural Addresses of the American Presidents* (NY: Holt, Rinehart and Winston, 1961), pp. 155-162. Charles E. Rice, *The Supreme Court and Public Prayer* (New York: Fordham University Press, 1964), p. 187. Arthur Schlesinger Jr., ed., *The Chief Executive* (NY: Chelsea House Publishers, 1965), pp. 171-179. Benjamin Weiss, *God in American History: A Documentation of America's Religious Heritage* (Grand Rapids, MI: Zondervan, 1966), p. 110. Willard Cantelon, *Money, Master of the World* (Plainfield, NJ: Logos International, 1976), p. 120. J. Michael Sharman, J.D., *Faith of the Fathers* (Culpepper, Virginia: Victory Publishing, 1995), p. 75.

[90] **Benjamin Harrison.** April 4, 1889, in a Proclamation of Prayer and Thanksgiving. James D. Richardson (U.S. Representative from Tennessee), ed., *A Compilation of the Messages and Papers of the Presidents 1789-1897*, 10 vols. (Washington, D.C.: U.S. Government Printing Office, published by Authority of Congress, 1897, 1899; Washington, D.C.: Bureau of National Literature and Art, *1789-1902*, 11 vols., 1907, 1910), Vol. IX, pp. 18-19.

[91] **Benjamin Harrison.** June 7, 1889, from his Executive Mansion. James D. Richardson (U.S. Representative from Tennessee), ed., *A Compilation of the Messages and Papers of the Presidents 1789-1897*, 10 vols. (Washington, D.C.: U.S. Government Printing Office, published by Authority of Congress, 1897, 1899; Washington, D.C.: Bureau of National Literature and Art, *1789-1902*, 11 vols., 1907, 1910), Vol. IX, p. 29.

[92] **Benjamin Harrison.** December 9, 1891, in his Third Annual Message. James D. Richardson (U.S. Representative from Tennessee), ed., *A Compilation of the Messages and Papers of the Presidents 1789-1897*, 10 vols. (Washington, D.C.: U.S. Government Printing Office, published by Authority of Congress, 1897, 1899; Washington, D.C.: Bureau of National Literature and Art, *1789-1902*, 11 vols., 1907, 1910), Vol. IX, pp. 188, 198.

[93] **(Stephen) Grover Cleveland.** March 4, 1893, Saturday, in his Second Inaugural Address. James D. Richardson (U.S. Representative from Tennessee), ed., *A Compilation of the Messages and Papers of the Presidents 1789-1897*, 10 vols. (Washington, D.C.: U.S. Government Printing Office, published by Authority of Congress, 1897, 1899; Washington, D.C.: Bureau of National Literature and Art, *1789-1902*, 11 vols., 1907, 1910), Vol. IX, pp. 389, 393. *Inaugural Addresses of the Presidents of the United States - From George Washington 1789 to Richard Milhous Nixon 1969* (Washington, D.C.: United States Government Printing Office; 91st Congress, 1st Session, House Document 91-142, 1969), pp. 163-167. Charles E. Rice, *The Supreme Court and Public Prayer* (New York: Fordham University Press, 1964), p. 187. Benjamin Weiss, *God in American History - A Documentation of America's Religious Heritage* (Grand Rapids, MI: Zondervan, 1966), p. 109. Willard Cantelon, *Money Master of the World* (Plainfield, NJ: Logos International, 1976), p. 120. J. Michael Sharman, J.D., *Faith of the Fathers* (Culpepper, Virginia: Victory Publishing, 1995), p. 77.

[94] **(Stephen) Grover Cleveland.** November 1, 1894, in a Proclamation of a National Day of Thanksgiving and Prayer. James D. Richardson (U.S. Representative from Tennessee), ed., *A Compilation of the Messages and Papers of the Presidents 1789-1897*, 10 vols. (Washington, D.C.: U.S. Government Printing Office, published by Authority of Congress, 1897, 1899; Washington, D.C.: Bureau of National Literature and Art, *1789-1902*, 11 vols., 1907, 1910), Vol. IX, p. 511.

[95] **(Stephen) Grover Cleveland.** December 2, 1895, in his Third Annual Message to Congress. James D. Richardson (U.S. Representative from Tennessee), ed., *A Compilation of the Messages and Papers of the Presidents 1789-1897*, 10 vols. (Washington, D.C.: U.S. Government Printing Office, published by Authority of Congress, 1897, 1899; Washington, D.C.: Bureau of National Literature and Art, *1789-1902*, 11 vols., 1907, 1910), Vol. IX, pp. 635, 637-638.

[96] **(Stephen) Grover Cleveland.** December 7, 1896, in his Fourth Annual Message, written to Congress from his Executive Mansion in Washington, D.C. James D. Richardson (U.S. Representative from Tennessee), ed., *A Compilation of the Messages and Papers of the Presidents 1789-1897*, 10 vols. (Washington, D.C.: U.S. Government Printing Office, published by Authority of Congress, 1897, 1899; Washington, D.C.: Bureau of National Literature and Art, *1789-1902*, 11 vols., 1907, 1910), Vol. IX, pp. 715-716.

[97] **William McKinley.** March 4, 1897, in his First Inaugural Address. *A Compilation of the Messages and Papers of the Presidents* 20 vols. (New York: Bureau of National Literature, Inc., prepared under the direction of the Joint Committee on Printing, of the House and Senate, pursuant to an Act of the Fifty-Second Congress of the United States, 1893, 1923), Vol. XIII, pp. 6236-6244. *Inaugural Addresses of the Presidents of the United States - From George Washington 1789 to Richard Milhous Nixon 1969* (Washington, D.C.: United States Government Printing Office; 91st Congress, 1st Session, House Document 91-142, 1969), pp. 169-177. Davis Newton Lott, *The Inaugural Addresses of the American Presidents* (NY: Holt, Rinehart and Winston, 1961), p. 171. Charles E. Rice, *The Supreme Court and Public Prayer* (New York: Fordham University Press, 1964), pp. 187-188. Arthur Schlesinger Jr., ed., *The Chief Executive* (NY: Chelsea House Publishers, 1965), p. 189. Benjamin Weiss, *God in American History: A Documentation of America's Religious Heritage* (Grand Rapids, MI: Zondervan, 1966) p. 115. Willard Cantelon, *Money Master of the World* (Plainfield, NJ: Logos International, 1976), p. 120. *Proclaim Liberty* (Dallas, TX: Word of Faith), p. 2. Stephen Abbott Northrop, D.D., *A Cloud of Witnesses* (Portland, OR: American Heritage Ministries, 1987; Mantle Ministries, 228 Still Ridge, Bulverde, Texas), p. 313. J. Michael Sharman, J.D., *Faith of the Fathers* (Culpepper, Virginia: Victory Publishing, 1995), p. 79.

[98] **William McKinley.** April 20, 1898, approved a Joint Resolution of Congress. James D. Richardson (U.S. Representative from Tennessee), ed., *A Compilation of the Messages and Papers of the Presidents 1789-1897*, 10 vols. (Washington, D.C.: U.S. Government Printing Office, published by Authority of Congress, 1897, 1899; Washington, D.C.: Bureau of National Literature and Art, *1789-1902*, 11 vols., 1907, 1910), Vol. X, p. 155.

[99] **William McKinley.** October 29, 1900, in a Proclamation of a National Day of Thanksgiving and Praise. *A Compilation of the Messages and Papers of the Presidents* 20 vols. (New York: Bureau of National Literature, Inc., prepared under the direction of the Joint Committee on Printing, of the House and Senate, pursuant to an Act of the Fifty-Second Congress of the United States, 1893, 1923), Vol. XIII, p. 6544.

[100] **William McKinley.** March 4, 1901, in his Second Inaugural Address. *A Compilation of the Messages and Papers of the Presidents* 20 vols. (New York: Bureau of National Literature, Inc., prepared under the direction of the Joint Committee on Printing, of the House and Senate, pursuant to an Act of the Fifty-Second Congress of the United States, 1893, 1923), Vol. XIII, pp. 6466-6467. *Inaugural Addresses of the Presidents of the United States - From George Washington 1789 to Richard Milhous Nixon 1969* (Washington, D.C.: United States Government Printing Office; 91st Congress, 1st Session, House Document 91-142, 1969), pp. 178-182. Davis Newton Lott, *The Inaugural Addresses of the American Presidents* (NY: Holt, Rinehart and Winston, 1961), p. 180. Charles E. Rice, *The Supreme Court and Public Prayer* (New York: Fordham University Press, 1964), p. 188. Arthur Schlesinger Jr., ed., *The Chief Executive* (NY: Chelsea House Publishers, 1965), pp. 199-200. J. Michael Sharman, J.D., *Faith of the Fathers* (Culpepper, Virginia: Victory Publishing, 1995), p. 80.

[101] **Theodore Roosevelt.** September 14, 1901, in a Proclamation of a National Day of Mourning and Prayer, issued at the occasion of President William McKinley's assassination. *A Compilation of the Messages and Papers of the Presidents* 20 vols. (New York: Bureau of National Literature, Inc., prepared under the direction of the Joint Committee on Printing, of the House and Senate, pursuant to an Act of the Fifty-Second Congress of the United States, 1893, 1923), Vol. XIII, p. 6639.

[102] **Theodore Roosevelt.** November 1, 1904, in a Proclamation of a National Day of Thanksgiving. *A Compilation of the Messages and Papers of the Presidents* 20 vols. (New York: Bureau of National Literature, Inc., prepared under the direction of the Joint Committee on Printing, of the House and Senate, pursuant to an Act of the Fifty-Second Congress of the United States, 1893, 1923), Vol. XIV, pp. 6889-6890.

[103] **Theodore Roosevelt.** December 6, 1904, in his Fourth Annual Message to Congress. *A Compilation of the Messages and Papers of the Presidents* 20 vols. (New York: Bureau of National Literature, Inc., prepared under the direction of the Joint Committee on Printing, of the House and Senate, pursuant to an Act of the Fifty-Second Congress of the United States, 1893, 1923), Vol. XIV, p. 6903, 6915-6916, 6921-6922, 6924-6925, 6928-6929.

[104] **Theodore Roosevelt.** March 4, 1905, in his Inaugural Address. *A Compilation of the Messages and Papers of the Presidents* 20 vols. (New York: Bureau of National Literature, Inc., prepared under the direction of the Joint Committee on Printing, of the House and Senate, pursuant to an Act of the Fifty-Second Congress of the United States, 1893, 1923), Vol. XIV, pp. 6930-6932. *Inaugural Addresses of the Presidents of the United States - From George Washington 1789 to Richard Milhous Nixon 1969* (Washington, D.C.: United States Government Printing Office; 91st Congress, 1st Session, House Document 91-142, 1969), pp. 183-185. Davis Newton Lott, *The Inaugural Addresses of the American Presidents* (NY: Holt, Rinehart and Winston, 1961), p. 188. Charles E. Rice, *The Supreme Court and Public Prayer* (New York: Fordham University Press, 1964), p. 188. *Proclaim Liberty* (Dallas, TX: Word of Faith), p. 2. J. Michael Sharman, J.D., *Faith of the Fathers* (Culpepper, Virginia: Victory Publishing, 1995), p. 82.

[105] **William Howard Taft.** March 4, 1909, in his Inaugural Address. *A Compilation of the Messages and Papers of the Presidents* 20 vols. (New York: Bureau of National Literature, Inc., prepared under the direction of the Joint Committee on Printing, of the House and Senate, pursuant to an Act of the Fifty-Second Congress of the United States, 1893, 1923), Vol. XV, p. 7379. *Inaugural Addresses of the Presidents of the United States - From George Washington 1789 to Richard Milhous Nixon 1969* (Washington, D.C.: United States Government Printing Office; 91st Congress, 1st Session, House Document 91-142, 1969), pp. 187-198. Charles E. Rice, *The Supreme Court and Public Prayer* (New York: Fordham University Press, 1964), pp. 188-189. Benjamin Weiss, *God in American History: A Documentation of America's Religious Heritage* (Grand Rapids, MI: Zondervan, 1966), p. 120. Willard Cantelon, *Money Master of the World* (Plainfield, NJ: Logos International, 1976), p. 121. Davis Newton Lott, *The Inaugural Addresses of the American Presidents* (NY: Holt, Rinehart and Winston, 1961), p. 197. J. Michael Sharman, J.D., *Faith of the Fathers* (Culpepper, Virginia: Victory Publishing, 1995), p. 84.

[106] **William Howard Taft.** November 7, 1912, in a Proclamation of a National Day of Thanksgiving. *A Compilation of the Messages and Papers of the Presidents* 20 vols. (New York: Bureau of National Literature, Inc., prepared under the direction of the Joint Committee on Printing, of the House and Senate, pursuant to an Act of the Fifty-Second Congress of the United States, 1893, 1923), Vol. XVI, pp. 7764-7765.

[107] **William Howard Taft.** November 15, 1909, in a Proclamation of a National Day of Thanksgiving. *A Compilation of the Messages and Papers of the Presidents* 20 vols. (New York: Bureau of National Literature, Inc., prepared under the direction of the Joint Committee on Printing, of the House and Senate, pursuant to an Act of the Fifty-Second Congress of the United States, 1893, 1923), Vol. XV, p. 7392.

[108] **William Howard Taft.** December 6, 1912, in his Annual Message to Congress, part II. *A Compilation of the Messages and Papers of the Presidents* 20 vols. (New York: Bureau of National Literature, Inc., prepared under the direction of the Joint Committee on Printing, of the House and Senate, pursuant to an Act of the Fifty-Second Congress of the United States, 1893, 1923), Vol. XVI, p. 7808.

[109] **(Thomas) Woodrow Wilson.** March 4, 1913 in his Inaugural Address. *A Compilation of the Messages and Papers of the Presidents* 20 vols. (New York: Bureau of National Literature, Inc., prepared under the direction of the Joint Committee on Printing, of the House and Senate, pursuant to an Act of the Fifty-Second Congress of the United States, 1893, 1923), Vol. XVI, p. 7871. *Inaugural Addresses of the Presidents of the United States - From George Washington 1789 to Richard Milhous Nixon 1969* (Washington, D.C.: United States Government Printing Office; 91st Congress, 1st Session, House Document 91-142, 1969), pp. 199-202. Ray Stannard Baker and William E. Dodd, eds., *The Public Papers of Woodrow Wilson* (New York and London, 1926), Vol. IV, p. 414. Paul M. Angle, *By These Words* (NY: Rand McNally & Company, 1954), p. 318. Davis Newton Lott, *The Inaugural Addresses of the American Presidents* (NY: Holt, Rinehart and Winston, 1961), p. 201. Charles E. Rice, *The Supreme Court and Public Prayer* (New York: Fordham University Press, 1964), p. 189. Benjamin Weiss, *God in American History: A Documentation of America's Religious Heritage* (Grand Rapids, MI: Zondervan, 1966), p. 125. Thomas A. Baily, *The American Pageant - A History of the Republic* (Lexington, MA: D.C. Heath and Company, 1971), p. 729. Willard Cantelon, *Money Master of the World* (Plainfield, NJ: Logos International, 1976), p. 125. Ronald Reid, ed., *Three Centuries of American Rhetorical Discourse - An Anthology and a Review* (Prospect Heights, IL: Waveland Press, Inc., 1988), p. 638. J. Michael Sharman, J.D., *Faith of the Fathers* (Culpepper, Virginia: Victory Publishing, 1995), p. 86.

[110] **(Thomas) Woodrow Wilson.** March 5, 1917, Monday, in his Second Inaugural Address, delivered on the front portico of the Capitol. *A Compilation of the Messages and Papers of the Presidents* 20 vols. (New York: Bureau of National Literature, Inc., prepared under the direction of the Joint Committee on Printing, of the House and Senate, pursuant to an Act of the Fifty-Second Congress of the United States, 1893, 1923), Vol. XVII, pp. 8221-8223. *Inaugural Addresses of the Presidents of the United States - From George Washington 1789 to Richard Milhous Nixon 1969* (Washington, D.C.: United States Government Printing Office; 91st Congress, 1st Session, House Document 91-142, 1969), pp. 203-206. Frederick C. Packard, Jr., ed., *Are You an American? - Great Americans Speak* (NY: Charles Scribner's Sons, 1951), p. 86. Davis Newton Lott, *The Inaugural Addresses of the American Presidents* (NY: Holt, Rinehart and Winston, 1961), p. 20. Charles E. Rice, *The Supreme Court and Public Prayer* (New York: Fordham University Press, 1964), p. 189. Benjamin Weiss, *God in American History: A Documentation of America's Religious Heritage* (Grand Rapids, MI: Zondervan, 1966), p. 125. Lillian W.Kay, ed., *The Ground on Which We Stand - Basic Documents of American History* (NY: Franklin Watts, Inc, 1969), p. 254. Willard Cantelon, *Money Master of the World* (Plainfield, NJ: Logos International, 1976), p. 125. *Proclaim Liberty* (Dallas, TX: Word of Faith), p. 2. William Safire, ed., *Lend Me Your Ears - Great Speeches in History* (NY: W.W. Norton & Company, 1992), p. 117. J. Michael Sharman, J.D., *Faith of the Fathers* (Culpepper, Virginia: Victory Publishing, 1995), p. 87.

[111] **(Thomas) Woodrow Wilson.** January 20, 1918, in an Executive Order to the Army and Navy enjoining Sabbath observance. *A Compilation of the Messages and Papers of the Presidents* 20 vols. (New York: Bureau of National Literature, Inc., prepared under the direction of the Joint Committee on Printing, of the House and Senate, pursuant to an Act of the Fifty-Second Congress of the United States, 1893, 1923), Vol. XVII, p. 8433.

[112] **(Thomas) Woodrow Wilson.** May 24, 1920, in a special message to Congress asking permission to assume the mandate for Armenia under the League of Nations. *A Compilation of the Messages and Papers of the Presidents* 20 vols. (New York: Bureau of National Literature, Inc., prepared under the direction of the Joint Committee on Printing, of the House and Senate, pursuant to an Act of the Fifty-Second Congress of the United States, 1893, 1923), Vol. XVIII, pp. 8853-8855.

[113] **Warren Gamaliel Harding.** March 4, 1921, Friday, in his Inaugural Address. *A Compilation of the Messages and Papers of the Presidents* 20 vols. (New York: Bureau of National Literature, Inc., prepared under the direction of the Joint Committee on Printing, of the House and Senate, pursuant to an Act of the Fifty-Second Congress of the United States, 1893, 1923), Vol. XVIII, pp. 8923-8930. *Inaugural Addresses of the Presidents of the United States - From George Washington 1789 to Richard Milhous Nixon 1969* (Washington, D.C.: United States Government Printing Office; 91st Congress, 1st Session, House Document 91-142, 1969), pp. 207-214. Charles E. Rice, *The Supreme Court and Public Prayer* (New York: Fordham University Press, 1964), pp. 189-190. Benjamin Weiss, *God in American History: A Documentation of America's Religious Heritage* (Grand Rapids, MI: Zondervan, 1966), p. 126. Willard Cantelon, *Money, Master of the World* (Plainfield, NJ: Logos International, 1976), p. 126. Davis Newton Lott, *The Inaugural Addresses of the American Presidents* (NY: Holt, Rinehart and Winston, 1961), p. 207. Arthur Schlesinger Jr., ed., *The Chief Executive* (NY: Chelsea House Publishers, 1965), pp. 232, 238. J. Michael Sharman, J.D., *Faith of the Fathers* (Culpepper, Virginia: Victory Publishing, 1995), pp. 89-90.

[114] **Warren Gamaliel Harding.** November 11, 1921, in addressing the Secretary of War and the citizens assembled at the burial of an Unknown American Soldier in Arlington Cemetery, Virginia. *A Compilation of the Messages and Papers of the Presidents* 20 vols. (New York: Bureau of National Literature, Inc., prepared under the direction of the Joint Committee on Printing, of the House and Senate, pursuant to an Act of the Fifty-Second Congress of the United States, 1893, 1923), Vol. XVIII, pp. 9010-9013.

[115] **Warren Gamaliel Harding.** June 21, 1923, in his address on the International Court of Justice, delivered in St. Louis, Missouri. *A Compilation of the Messages and Papers of the Presidents* 20 vols. (New York: Bureau of National Literature, Inc., prepared under the direction of the Joint Committee on Printing, of the House and Senate, pursuant to an Act of the Fifty-Second Congress of the United States, 1893, 1923), Vol. XVIII, pp. 9240-9248.

[116] **Warren Gamaliel Harding.** July 3, 1923, in a speech about the Oregon Trail given at Meacham, Oregon. "Harding, Warren Gamaliel; A Government Document," Washington, D.C.: Government Printing Office, 1923. *A Compilation of the Messages and Papers of the Presidents* 20 vols. (New York: Bureau of National Literature, Inc., prepared under the direction of the Joint Committee on Printing, of the House and Senate, pursuant to an Act of the Fifty-Second Congress of the United States, 1893, 1923), Vol. XVIII, pp. 9299-9303. Catherine Millard, *The Rewriting of America's History* (Camp Hill, PA: Horizon House Publishers, 1991), pp. 208-211.

[117] **(John) Calvin Coolidge.** August 4, 1923, in a Proclamation of a National Day of Mourning and Prayer issued from the White House. *A Compilation of the Messages and Papers of the Presidents* 20 vols. (New York: Bureau of National Literature, Inc., prepared under the direction of the Joint Committee on Printing, of the House and Senate, pursuant to an Act of the Fifty-Second Congress of the United States, 1893, 1923), Vol. XVIII, pp. 9321-9322.

[118] **(John) Calvin Coolidge.** March 4, 1925, in his Inaugural Address. *Inaugural Addresses of the Presidents of the United States - From George Washington 1789 to Richard Milhous Nixon 1969* (Washington, D.C.: United States Government Printing Office; 91st Congress, 1st Session, House Document 91-142, 1969), pp. 215-223. Calvin Coolidge, *Foundations of the Republic - Speeches and Addresses* (New York: Charles Scribner's Sons, 1926), p. 205. McCollister, *So Help Me God*, p. 137. Charles E. Rice, *The Supreme Court and Public Prayer* (New York: Fordham University Press, 1964), p. 190. Benjamin Weiss, *God in American History: A Documentation of America's Religious Heritage* (Grand Rapids, MI: Zondervan, 1966), p. 131. Lott, ed., *The Inaugural Addresses of the American Presidents*, p. 221. Reid, ed., *Three Centuries of American Rhetorical Discourse*, p. 667. Willard Cantelon, *Money Master of the World* (Plainfield, NJ: Logos International, 1976), p. 191. Peter Marshall and David Manuel, *The Glory of America* (Bloomington, MN: Garborg's Heart 'N Home, Inc., 1991), 1.4. *Proclaim Liberty* (Dallas, Tx: Word of Faith), p. 2. J. Michael Sharman, J.D., *Faith of the Fathers* (Culpepper, Virginia: Victory Publishing, 1995), pp. 92-93.

[119] **(John) Calvin Coolidge.** September 21, 1924, in an address to the Holy Name Society, Washington, D.C. Calvin Coolidge, *Foundations of the Republic - Speeches and Addresses* (New York: Charles Scribner's Sons, 1926), pp. 103-112.

[120] **(John) Calvin Coolidge.** May 3, 1925, at the laying on the cornerstone of the Jewish Community Center, Washington, D.C. Calvin Coolidge, *Foundations of the Republic - Speeches and Addresses* (New York: Charles Scribner's Sons, 1926), pp. 209-218.

[121] **Herbert Clark Hoover.** March 4, 1929, Monday, in his Inaugural Address. *Inaugural Addresses of the Presidents of the United States - From George Washington 1789 to Richard Milhous Nixon 1969* (Washington, D.C.: United States Government Printing Office; 91st Congress, 1st Session, House Document 91-142, 1969), pp. 225-233. Davis Newton Lott, *The Inaugural Addresses of the American Presidents* (NY: Holt, Rinehart and Winston, 1961), pp. 223, 229. Charles E. Rice, *The Supreme*

Court and Public Prayer (New York: Fordham University Press, 1964), pp. 190-191. Arthur Schlesinger Jr., ed., *The Chief Executive* (NY: Chelsea House Publishers, 1965), pp. 250, 259. Benjamin Weiss, *God in American History: A Documentation of America's Religious Heritage* (Grand Rapids, MI: Zondervan, 1966), p. 132. Willard Cantelon, *Money Master of the World* (Plainfield, NJ: Logos International, 1976), p. 121. J. Michael Sharman, J.D., *Faith of the Fathers* (Culpepper, Virginia: Victory Publishing, 1995), p. 95.

[102] **Herbert Clark Hoover.** April 27, 1931, in an address before the Gridiron Club. Herbert Hoover, *The Memoirs of Herbert Hoover - The Great Depression 1929-1941* (New York: The MacMillan Company, 1952), p. 64.

[103] **Herbert Clark Hoover.** October 18, 1931, in an address beginning a nation-wide drive to aid the private relief agencies during the Great Depression. Herbert Hoover, *The Memoirs of Herbert Hoover - The Great Depression 1929-1941* (New York: The MacMillan Company, 1952), p. 151.

[104] **Herbert Clark Hoover.** September 15, 1932, in addressing the leaders of the "national drive" committee for voluntary relief agencies at the White House. Herbert Hoover, *The Memoirs of Herbert Hoover - The Great Depression 1929-1941* (New York: The MacMillan Company, 1952), pp. 174-175.

[105] **Franklin Delano Roosevelt.** March 4, 1933, in his First Inaugural Address. *Inaugural Addresses of the Presidents of the United States - From George Washington 1789 to Richard Milhous Nixon 1969* (Washington, D.C.: United States Government Printing Office; 91st Congress, 1st Session, House Document 91-142, 1969), pp. 235-239. Richard D. Heffner, *A Documentary History of the United States* (New York: The New American Library of World Literature, Inc., 1961), p. 270. Davis Newton Lott, *The Inaugural Addresses of the American Presidents* (NY: Holt, Rinehart and Winston, 1961), p. 234. Charles E. Rice, *The Supreme Court and Public Prayer* (New York: Fordham University Press, 1964), p. 191. Benjamin Weiss, *God in American History: A Documentation of America's Religious Heritage* (Grand Rapids, MI: Zondervan, 1966), pp. 137-138. John Bartlett, *Bartlett's Familiar Quotations* (Boston: Little, Brown and Company, 1855, 1980), p. 779. Lillian W. Kay, ed., *The Ground on Which We Stand - Basic Documents of American History* (NY: Franklin Watts., Inc, 1969), #257. Willard Cantelon, *Money Master of the World* (Plainfield, NJ: Logos International, 1976), p. 121. William Safire, ed., *Lend Me Your Ears - Great Speeches in History* (NY: W.W. Norton & Company 1992), p. 783. J. Michael Sharman, J.D., *Faith of the Fathers* (Culpepper, Virginia: Victory Publishing, 1995), p. 97.

[106] **Franklin Delano Roosevelt.** January 20, 1937, in his Second Inaugural Address. *Inaugural Addresses of the Presidents of the United States - From George Washington 1789 to Richard Milhous Nixon 1969* (Washington, D.C.: United States Government Printing Office; 91st Congress, 1st Session, House Document 91-142, 1969), pp. 240-243. Charles E. Rice, *The Supreme Court and Public Prayer* (New York: Fordham University Press, 1964), p. 191. Benjamin Weiss, *God in American History: A Documentation of America's Religious Heritage* (Grand Rapids, MI: Zondervan, 1966), pp. 137-138. Davis Newton Lott, *The Inaugural Addresses of the American Presidents* (NY: Holt, Rinehart and Winston, 1961), p. 240. Willard Cantelon, *Money Master of the World* (Plainfield, NJ: Logos International, 1976), p. 121. J. Michael Sharman, J.D., *Faith of the Fathers* (Culpepper, Virginia: Victory Publishing, 1995), p. 98.

[107] **Franklin Delano Roosevelt.** January 20, 1941, Third Inaugural Address. *Inaugural Addresses of the Presidents of the United States - From George Washington 1789 to Richard Milhous Nixon 1969* (Washington, D.C.: United States Government Printing Office; 91st Congress, 1st Session, House Document 91-142, 1969), pp. 244-247. Charles E. Rice, *The Supreme Court and Public Prayer* (New York: Fordham University Press, 1964), p. 191. Benjamin Weiss, *God in American History: A Documentation of America's Religious Heritage* (Grand Rapids, MI: Zondervan, 1966), pp. 137-138. Willard Cantelon, *Money Master of the World* (Plainfield, NJ: Logos International, 1976), p. 121. J. Michael Sharman, J.D., *Faith of the Fathers* (Culpepper, Virginia: Victory Publishing, 1995), p. 99.

[108] **Franklin Delano Roosevelt.** January 20, 1945, Saturday, in his Fourth Inaugural Address, delivered on the Portico of the White House. *Inaugural Addresses of the Presidents of the United States - From George Washington 1789 to Richard Milhous Nixon 1969* (Washington, D.C.: United States Government Printing Office; 91st Congress, 1st Session, House Document 91-142, 1969), pp. 248-249. Davis Newton Lott, *The Inaugural Addresses of the American Presidents* (NY: Holt, Rinehart and Winston, 1961), pp. 247-248. Charles E. Rice, *The Supreme Court and Public Prayer* (New York: Fordham University Press, 1964), p. 191. Benjamin Weiss, *God in American History: A Documentation of America's Religious Heritage* (Grand Rapids, MI: Zondervan, 1966), pp. 137-138. Willard Cantelon, *Money Master of the World* (Plainfield, NJ: Logos International, 1976), p. 121. *Proclaim Liberty* (Dallas, TX: Word of Faith), p. 2. J. Michael Sharman, J.D., *Faith of the Fathers* (Culpepper, Virginia: Victory Publishing, 1995), p. 100.

[129] **Harry S. Truman.** April 12, 1945, in his first address to Congress as President. Merle Miller, *Plain Speaking - An Oral Biography of Harry S. Truman* (Berkley, 1982). Charles E. Jones, *The Books You Read* (Harrisburg, PA: Executive Books, 1985), p. 197. Edmund Fuller and David E. Green, *God in the White House - The Faiths of American Presidents* (NY: Crown Publishers, Inc., 1968), p. 210.

[130] **Harry S. Truman.** December 24, 1946, in an address given at the Ceremony for the lighting of the national Christmas tree. T.S. Settel, and the staff of *Quote*, editors, *The Quotable Harry Truman* introduction by Merle Miller (NY: Droke House Publishers, Inc., Berkley Publishing Corporation, 1967), pp. 44, 57, 82, 115.

[131] **Harry S. Truman.** November 29, 1948, in a personal letter to Dr. Chaim Weizmann, President of the State of Israel. Harry S. Truman, *Memoirs by Harry S. Truman - Volume Two: Years of Trial and Hope* (Garden City, NY: Doubleday & Company, Inc., 1956), pp. 168-169.

[132] **Harry S. Truman.** January 20, 1949, in his Inaugural Address. Harry S. Truman, *Memoirs by Harry S. Truman - Volume Two: Years of Trial and Hope* (Garden City, NY: Doubleday & Company, Inc., 1956), pp. 226-227. *Inaugural Addresses of the Presidents of the United States - From George Washington 1789 to Richard Milhous Nixon 1969* (Washington, D.C.: United States Government Printing Office; 91st Congress, 1st Session, House Document 91-142, 1969), pp. 251-256. Davis Newton Lott, *The Inaugural Addresses of the American Presidents* (NY: Holt, Rinehart and Winston, 1961), pp. 251-255. Charles E. Rice, *The Supreme Court and Public Prayer* (New York: Fordham University Press, 1964), pp. 191-192. Lillian W. Kay, ed., *The Ground on Which We Stand - Basic Documents of American History* (NY: Franklin Watts., Inc, 1969), p. 275. Benjamin Weiss, *God in American History: A Documentation of America's Religious Heritage* (Grand Rapids, MI: Zondervan, 1966), p. 141. Willard Cantelon, *Money Master of the World* (Plainfield, NJ: Logos International, 1976), p. 121. *Proclaim Liberty* (Dallas, TX: Word of Faith), p. 2. J. Michael Sharman, J.D., *Faith of the Fathers* (Culpepper, Virginia: Victory Publishing, 1995), pp. 102-104. T.S. Settel, and the staff of *Quote*, editors, *The Quotable Harry Truman* introduction by Merle Miller (NY: Droke House Publishers, Inc., Berkley Publishing Corporation, 1967), p. 76.

[133] **Dwight David Eisenhower.** January 20, 1953, in his Inaugural Address. *New York Times*, January 21, 1953. *Inaugural Addresses of the Presidents of the United States - From George Washington 1789 to Richard Milhous Nixon 1969* (Washington, D.C.: United States Government Printing Office; 91st Congress, 1st Session, House Document 91-142, 1969), pp. 257-262. Paul M. Angle, ed., *By These Words* (NY: Rand McNally & Company, 1954), pp. 400-408. Davis Newton Lott, *The Inaugural Addresses of the American Presidents* (NY: Holt, Rinehart and Winston, 1961), pp. 257-261. Charles Hurd, ed., *A Treasury of Great American Speeches* (NY: Hawthorne Books, 1959), (paragraphs 2-4), pp. 305-306. D.D. Eisenhower, *The Inaugural Prayer* (Denison, TX: on display at the Eisenhower Birthplace Memorial, 208 E. Day, Denison, Texas, 75020). Charles E. Rice, *The Supreme Court and Public Prayer* (New York: Fordham University Press, 1964), pp. 192-193. Edmund Fuller and David E. Green, *God in the White House - The Faiths of American Presidents* (NY: Crown Publishers, Inc., 1968), p. 217. Edward L.R. Elson, D.D., Lit.D., LL.D., *America's Spiritual Recovery* (Westwood, N.J.: Fleming H. Revell Company, 1954), p. 56. January 20, 1953, Scripture choice at his Inauguration, January 20, 1953: "If my people, who are called by my name, will humble themselves and pray and seek my face, and turn from their wicked ways, then I will hear from heaven, will forgive their sin, and heal their land."(II Chronicles 7:14). Catherine Millard, *The Rewriting of America's History* (Camp Hill, PA: Horizon House Publishers, 1991), p. 204. J. Michael Sharman, J.D., *Faith of the Fathers* (Culpepper, Virginia: Victory Publishing, 1995), pp. 106-108.

[134] **Dwight David Eisenhower.** October 31, 1953, in a program produced by the Committee on Religion in American Life, broadcast nationally via radio and television. *Public Papers of the Presidents - Dwight D. Eisenhower, 1953 - Containing Public Messages, Speeches, and Statements of the President, January 20 to December 31, 1953* (Washington, DC: United States Government Printing Office, 1960), Item 236, p. 736.

[135] **Dwight David Eisenhower.** November 9, 1954, to the first National Conference on the Spiritual Foundation of American Democracy in a luncheon meeting at the Sheraton-Carlton Hotel in Washington, DC. *Public Papers of the Presidents - Dwight D. Eisenhower, 1954 - Containing Public Messages, Speeches, and Statements of the President, January 1 to December 31, 1954* (Washington, DC: United States Government Printing Office, 1960), Item 327, p. 1029-31.

[136] **Dwight David Eisenhower.** January 21, 1957, Monday, in his Second Inaugural Address. *Inaugural Addresses of the Presidents of the United States - From George Washington 1789 to Richard Milhous Nixon 1969* (Washington, D.C.: United States Government Printing Office; 91st Congress, 1st Session, House Document 91-142, 1969), pp. 263-266. Benjamin Weiss, *God in American History: A Documentation of America's Religious Heritage* (Grand Rapids, MI: Zondervan, 1966), p. 145. Davis Newton Lott, *The Inaugural Addresses of the American Presidents* (NY: Holt, Rinehart and Winston, 1961), p. 263. Charles E. Rice, *The Supreme Court and Public Prayer*

(New York: Fordham University Press, 1964), p. 193. Charles Wallis, ed., *Our American Heritage* (NY: Harper & Row, Publishers, Inc., 1970), p. 54. Willard Cantelon, *Money Master of the World* (Plainfield, NJ: Logos International, 1976), p. 121. *Proclaim Liberty* (Dallas, TX: Word of Faith), p. 3. J. Michael Sharman, J.D., *Faith of the Fathers* (Culpepper, Virginia: Victory Publishing, 1995), p. 109.

[137] **John Fitzgerald Kennedy.** January 20, 1961, Friday, in his Inaugural Address. *Inaugural Addresses of the Presidents of the United States - From George Washington 1789 to Richard Milhous Nixon 1969* (Washington, D.C.: United States Government Printing Office; 91st Congress, 1st Session, House Document 91-142, 1969), pp. 267-270. Davis Newton Lott, *The Inaugural Addresses of the American Presidents* (NY: Holt, Rinehart and Winston, 1961), p. 269. Charles E. Rice, *The Supreme Court and Public Prayer* (New York: Fordham University Press, 1964), p. 193. Benjamin Weiss, *God in American History: A Documentation of America's Religious Heritage* (Grand Rapids, MI: Zondervan, 1966), p. 146. *The Annals of America*, 20 vols. (Chicago, IL: Encyclopedia Britannica, 1968), Vol. XVIII, p. 7. Lillian W. Kay, ed., *The Ground on Which We Stand - Basic Documents of American History* (NY: Franklin Watts., Inc, 1969), p. 296. Willard Cantelon, *Money Master of the World* (Plainfield, NJ: Logos International, 1976), p. 121-122. Bob Arnebeck, "FDR Invoked God Too," *Washington Post*, September 21, 1986. Vincent J. Wilson, ed., *The Book of Great American Documents* (Brookfield, MD: American History Research Associates, 1987), p. 84. Halford Ross Ryan, *American Rhetoric from Roosevelt to Reagan* (Prospect Heights, IL: Waveland Press, 1987), p. 156. Jeffrey K. Hadden and Anson Shupe, *Televangelism - Power & Politics on God's Frontier* (NY: Henry Holt and Company, 1988), p. 272. Ronald Reid, ed., *Three Centuries of American Rhetorical Discourse: An Anthology and a Review* (Prospect Heights, Il: Waveland Press, Inc., 1988), p. 711. William Safire, ed., *Lend Me Your Ears - Great Speeches in History* (NY: W.W. Norton & Company 1992), p. 812. Peter Marshall and David Manuel, *The Glory of America* (Bloomington, MN: Garborg's Heart 'N Home, Inc., 1991), 1.20. *Proclaim Liberty* (Dallas, TX: Word of Faith), p. 3. J. Michael Sharman, J.D., *Faith of the Fathers* (Culpepper, Virginia: Victory Publishing, 1995), pp. 111-112.

[138] **John Fitzgerald Kennedy.** November 16, 1961, at the University of Washington. "Diplomacy and Defense: A Test of National Maturity," *Department of State Bulletin* (published weekly by the Office of Public Services, Bureau of Public Affairs, December 4, 1961). *The Annals of America* 20 Vols. (Chicago, IL: Encyclopedia Britannica, Inc., 1976), Vol. 18, pp. 54-57.

[139] **John Fitzgerald Kennedy.** July 11, 1963, in a radio and television address to the Nation. *Congressional Record*, 88th Congress, 1st Session, pp. 10965-10966. *The Annals of America* 20 Vols. (Chicago, IL: Encyclopedia Britannica, Inc., 1976), Vol. 18, pp. 152-155.

[140] **John Fitzgerald Kennedy.** November 22, 1963, the conclusion to the speech he had prepared to give at the Dallas Trade Mart, before he was assassinated. *Congressional Record*, 88th Congress, 1st Session, pp. 22823-22824. *The Annals of America*, 20 vols. (Chicago, IL: Encyclopedia Britannica, 1968), Vol. XVIII, p. 201. Peter Marshall and David Manuel, *The Glory of America* (Bloomington, MN: Garborg's Heart'N Home, Inc., 1991), 11.22.

[141] **Lyndon Baines Johnson.** November 27, 1963, in his first formal address before a joint session of Congress, with members of the Supreme Court and of the Cabinet in attendance. *Congressional Record*, 88th Congress, 1st Session, pp. 22838-22839. *The Annals of America* 20 Vols. (Chicago, IL: Encyclopedia Britannica, Inc., 1976), Vol. 18, pp. 203-206.

[142] **Lyndon Baines Johnson.** January 20, 1965, Wednesday, in his Inaugural Address. *Inaugural Addresses of the Presidents of the United States - From George Washington 1789 to Richard Milhous Nixon 1969* (Washington, D.C.: United States Government Printing Office; 91st Congress, 1st Session, House Document 91-142, 1969), pp. 271-274. Benjamin Weiss, *God in American History: A Documentation of America's Religious Heritage* (Grand Rapids, MI: Zondervan, 1966), p. 151. Willard Cantelon, *Money Master of the World* (Plainfield, NJ: Logos International, 1976), p. 122. *Proclaim Liberty* (Dallas, TX: Word of Faith), p. 3. J. Michael Sharman, J.D., *Faith of the Fathers* (Culpepper, Virginia: Victory Publishing, 1995), p. 114.

[143] **Lyndon Baines Johnson.** In explaining his support for the Model Cities Act, passed by Congress in September of 1966. Lyndon Baines Johnson, *The Vantage Point - Perspectives of the Presidency 1963-1969* (New York: Holt, Rinehart and Winston, 1971), p. 329.

[144] **Lyndon Baines Johnson.** Sunday, March 31, 1968, at 9:01 p.m., in a television broadcast from the Oval Office. *Chicago Sun-Times*, April 1, 1968. *The Annals of America* 20 Vols. (Chicago, IL: Encyclopedia Britannica, Inc., 1976), Vol. 18, pp. 613-616. Lyndon Baines Johnson, *The Vantage Point - Perspectives of the Presidency 1963-1969* (New York: Holt, Rinehart and Winston, 1971), p. 435.

[145] **Richard Milhous Nixon.** January 20, 1969, Monday, in his Inaugural Address. *Department of State Bulletin,* February 10, 1969. *Inaugural Addresses of the Presidents - From George Washington 1789 to Richard Milhous Nixon 1969* (Washington, D.C.: United States Government Printing Office, 91st Congress, 1st Session, House Document 91-142, 1969), pp. 275-279. *The Annals of America,* 20 vols. (Chicago, IL: Encyclopedia Britannica, 1968, 1977), Vol. 19, pp. 8-12. Benjamin Weiss, *God in American History: A Documentation of America's Religious Heritage* (Grand Rapids, MI: Zondervan, 1966), p. 154. Willard Cantelon, *Money Master of the World* (Plainfield, NJ: Logos International, 1976), p. 122. J. Michael Sharman, J.D., *Faith of the Fathers* (Culpeper, Virginia: Victory Publishing, 1995), pp. 116-117.

[146] **Richard Milhous Nixon.** January, 20, 1973, Saturday, in his Second Inaugural Address. J. Michael Sharman, J.D., *Faith of the Fathers* (Culpepper, Virginia: Victory Publishing, 1995), p. 118.

[147] **Richard Milhous Nixon.** August 8, 1974, Thursday, in a televised address to the nation announcing his resignation from office. *Weekly Compilation of Presidential Documents,* August 12, 1974. *The Annals of America,* 20 vols. (Chicago, IL: Encyclopedia Britannica, 1968, 1977), Vol. 20, pp. 22-25.

[148] **Richard Milhous Nixon.** August 8, 1974, Thursday, in a private farewell to the members of the White House Staff and friends. *Weekly Compilation of Presidential Documents,* August 12, 1974. *The Annals of America,* 20 vols. (Chicago, IL: Encyclopedia Britannica, 1968, 1977), Vol. 20, pp. 25-27.

[149] **Gerald Rudolph Ford.** August 9, 1974, after swearing in as the 38th President of the United States, in an address to Chief Justice Warren E. Burger, members of Congress and the citizens of America. *Weekly Compilation of Presidential Documents,* August 12, 1974. *The Annals of America,* 20 vols. (Chicago, IL: Encyclopedia Britannica, 1968, 1977), Vol. 20, pp. 30-32. Benjamin Weiss, *God in American History: A Documentation of America's Religious Heritage* (Grand Rapids, MI: Zondervan, 1966), p. 158. Willard Cantelon, *Money Master of the World* (Plainfield, NJ: Logos International, 1976), p. 122.

[150] **Gerald Rudolph Ford.** August 12, 1974, in his First Address to Congress. *Weekly Compilation of Presidential Documents,* August 19, 1974. *The Annals of America,* 20 vols. (Chicago, IL: Encyclopedia Britannica, 1968, 1977), Vol. 20, pp. 32-33.

[151] **Gerald Rudolph Ford.** September 8, 1974, Sunday, in announcing his decision to pardon former President Nixon. *Weekly Compilation of Presidential Documents,* September 16, 1974. *The Annals of America,* 20 vols. (Chicago, IL: Encyclopedia Britannica, 1968, 1977), Vol. 20, pp. 36-37.

[152] **Gerald Rudolph Ford.** December 5, 1974, Thursday, in a Proclamation of a National Day of Prayer, Proclamation 4338, quoting from a 1955 speech of Dwight David Eisenhower. Mrs. James Dobson (Shirley), chairman, *The National Day of Prayer Information Packet* (Colorado Springs, CO: National Day of Prayer Tack Force, May 6, 1993).

[153] **James Earl "Jimmy" Carter, Jr.** January 20, 1977, Thursday, in his Inaugural Address. "Our Christian Heritage," *Letter from Plymouth Rock* (Marlborough, NH: The Plymouth Rock Foundation), p. 7. J. Michael Sharman, J.D., *Faith of the Fathers* (Culpepper, Virginia: Victory Publishing, 1995), p. 121.

[154] **James Earl "Jimmy" Carter, Jr.** January 20, 1977, Thursday, in his Inaugural Address. "Our Christian Heritage," *Letter from Plymouth Rock* (Marlborough, NH: The Plymouth Rock Foundation), p. 7. J. Michael Sharman, J.D., *Faith of the Fathers* (Culpepper, Virginia: Victory Publishing, 1995), p. 121.

[155] **James Earl "Jimmy" Carter, Jr.** July 15, 1976, Thursday, in his Democratic acceptance speech, delivered in Madison Square Garden, New York City. *Vital Speeches,* August 15, 1976. *The Annals of America,* 20 vols. (Chicago, IL: Encyclopedia Britannica, 1968, 1977), Vol. 20, pp. 348-351.

[156] **James Earl "Jimmy" Carter, Jr.** March 16, 1976, in an interview with Robert L. Turner. John Bartlett, *Bartlett's Familiar Quotations* (Boston: Little, Brown and Company, 1855, 1980), p. 903.

[157] **Ronald Wilson Reagan.** January 20, 1981, Tuesday, in his inaugural address. *Congressional Quarterly,* "President Reagan," 1981, p. 115. Pat Robertson, *America's Dates with Destiny* (Nashville: Thomas Nelson Publishers, 1986), p. 285. J. Michael Sharman, J.D., *Faith of the Fathers* (Culpeper, Virginia: Victory Publishing, 1995), p. 123.

[158] **Ronald Wilson Reagan.** October 4, 1982, signed into law *Public Law 97-280,* as authorized and requested by a Joint Resolution of the Senate and House in the 97th Congress of the United States of America, held at the City of Washington. "Our Christian Heritage," *Letter from Plymouth Rock* (Marlborough, NH: The Plymouth Rock Foundation), p. 7. Public Law 97-280, 96 Stat. 1211. Gary DeMar, *America's Christian History: The Untold Story* (Atlanta, GA: American Vision Publishers, Inc., 1993), p. 53. John Eidsmoe, *Christianity and The Constitution - The Faith of Our Founding Fathers* (Grand Rapids, MI: Baker Book House, 1987), p. 355.

Tyndale House Publishers, Inc., 1984), pp. 68-69.

[160] **Ronald Wilson Reagan.** January 21, 1985, Monday, in his Second Inaugural Address. J. Michael Sharman, J.D., *Faith of the Fathers* (Culpepper, Virginia: Victory Publishing, 1995), pp. 124-125. Frederick J. Ryan, Jr., ed., *Ronald Reagan - The Wisdom and Humor of The Great Communicator* (San Francisco: Collins Publishers, A Division of Harper Collins Publishers, 1995), p. 12.

[161] **George Herbert Walker Bush.** January 20, 1989, Friday, in his Inaugural Address. J. Michael Sharman, J.D., *Faith of the Fathers* (Culpepper, Virginia: Victory Publishing, 1995), p. 127.

[162] **George Herbert Walker Bush.** February 22, 1990, in a Presidential Proclamation declaring 1990 the *International Year of Bible Reading,* concurring with the request of Congress, Senate Joint Resolution 164. Courtesy of Bruce Barilla, Christian Heritage Week Ministry (P.O. Box 58, W.V. 24712; 304-384-7707, 304-384-9044 fax).

[163] **George Herbert Walker Bush.** May 3, 1990, in a *Proclamation of a National Day of Prayer.* "Our Christian Heritage," *Letter from Plymouth Rock* (Marlborough, NH: The Plymouth Rock Foundation), p. 8.

[164] **George Herbert Walker Bush.** 1992, in a *Proclamation of a National Day of Prayer.* Mrs. James Dobson (Shirley), chairman, *The Annual National Day of Prayer* (Colorado Springs, CO: National Day of Prayer, 1993).

[165] **William Jefferson "Bill" Clinton.** January 20, 1993, in his Inaugural Address. J. Michael Sharman, J.D., *Faith of the Fathers* (Culpepper, Virginia: Victory Publishing, 1995), pp. 129-130..

[166] **William Jefferson "Bill" Clinton.** July 12, 1995, Wednesday, in an address at the James Madison High School in Vienna, Virginia, a suburb of Washington, D.C. Kathy Lewis and Cara Tanamachi, *Washington Bureau of the Dallas Morning News,* "Clinton orders guidelines on school religious issues - President wants to head off GOP prayer amendment" *The Dallas Morning News* (Dallas, TX: The Dallas Morning News, Inc., A.H. Belo Corporation, Thursday, July 13, 1995), pp. 1A, 10A.